W9-AVB-351

Contents

NUMBERS
Don't Lie

THE BIGGEST NUMBERS IN DETROIT TIGERS HISTORY

World Championships	Pennants	Playoff Appearances
 4	 11	 16

Danny Knobler

TRIUMPH
BOOKS

This book is available in quantity at special discounts for your group or organization. For further information, contact:

Triumph Books LLC
814 North Franklin Street
Chicago, Illinois 60610
(312) 337–0747
www.triumphbooks.com

Printed in U.S.A.

ISBN: 978-1-62937-090-3

Design by Andy Hansen
Production by Patricia Frey

Photos courtesy of Getty Images except where otherwise noted.

Foreword

It was Tuesday afternoon and I was sitting in my library contemplating the 2014 season, and its abrupt end brought about by the Baltimore Orioles and my transition to civilian life when the phone rang. Now this was my private line that not many people have and although I wasn't quite done anguishing over the season's end, I answered. It was Danny. He asked if I would take a look at his new book about our Tigers. I've looked over hundreds of sports books and Danny asked if I would write a foreword for him. My first thought went back to what my great friend Ernie—Ernie Harwell—told me some years ago. Ernie said that so much has been written about sports, in order for a sports book to be "good" it must be "unique." With that in mind, I told Danny I'd give it a go.

The title piqued my interest almost immediately. Baseball has long been a game of numbers. From batting averages and winning percentages to walks, hits, innings pitched, and on-base percentage, baseball has been understood through and by the numbers. It is the quintessential game of stats. As a player, those numbers were an integral part of my life. I needed to know stats on pitchers and hitters as I called games when catching. As a commentator I continue to use those numbers to help fans understand and visualize what is happening on the field. In fact, you've probably heard me say on the air that a certain number will trigger memories that just seem to pop into my head. Twenty-four is certainly Miguel Cabrera, but for me it's Mickey Stanley too. So reading a book about the Tigers' numbers intrigued me.

Approaching Tiger history through numbers certainly meets Ernie's criteria of being unique and I'm happy to add, refreshing too. Danny gives those numbers historical perspective by moving back and forth between the past and the present. He helps to bring life to some of those statues out behind center field. Tiger fans, the best fans ever known, are going to "eat this book up." It's not only a story and a history, but a reference too. As much a cliché as it is, there truly is something for everyone in this book. It has a universal appeal as it crosses generations and ties the past to the present. Fans will love to make this part of their personal "arsenal." I'm happy to have written this foreword and I'm certainly glad I answered that phone. "Good call," Danny.

—Jim Price
No. 12

Introduction

If you grew up with the Tigers, you grew up with numbers.

For one generation, it's 35–5. For another, it's 31.

Maybe you're a little older, and it's Hank Greenberg hitting 58. Or maybe your grandfather (or your grandfather's grandfather) reminded you regularly that Ty Cobb hit .367.

Or it's Justin Verlander throwing two no-hitters, or Miguel Cabrera ending baseball's 45-year wait for a Triple Crown.

For me, it was 51, because in my first season on the Tiger beat for Booth Newspapers, Cecil Fielder hit 51 home runs. Forever, 51 would mean Cecil Fielder, just as 31 always means Denny McLain, and 35–5 always means 1984.

The idea for this book is to tell Tiger history through the numbers you remember, and even a few you don't. The idea is to present the best players and teams the Tigers have ever had (and even some of the worst) through the numbers they compiled, the numbers they made memorable.

We didn't deal with year numbers like 1984 or 1968, but we sure did deal with those seasons and more. We didn't use uniform numbers, even though any Tiger fan would recognize 6 as Al Kaline, and would know that Cobb never had any number at all on his back.

We did deal with the three straight American League pennants in the Cobb era, and with the four playoff appearances in eight years under Jim Leyland in the era that featured Verlander and Cabrera.

We dealt with Tiger Stadium, and with Comerica Park. We have Ernie Harwell broadcasting something like 6,000 Tiger games, and Kaline staying with the Tigers for 62 years (and counting).

We have Bill Lajoie's drafts and Dave Dombrowski's trades. We have 119 losses in 2003, but also the 12 players from that team who were part of a World Series team just three seasons later.

The Tigers have played in the American League for 114 seasons, so it's impossible to cover everything. It's impossible to mention every team and every player (and there are probably a few you'd just as soon we leave out).

Sure, there were some lean years. But as any Tiger fan could tell you, they've had their share of great ones, too.

"History was my favorite subject in school," Alan Trammell told author George Cantor a few years back. "I know the Yankees have their tradition and I bow to what they have accomplished over the years. But the Detroit Tigers don't have to take a back seat to anyone when it comes to tradition."

Trammell was part of it, and his decision never to play for another team gave him and his double-play partner Lou Whitaker a record that no other team can match. Trammell has worn other uniforms as a coach, but his connection to the Tigers and their fans will never be broken.

He's always the guy who had nine hits in the 1984 World Series, just as Kaline is always the guy who won a batting title at age 20, just as Mickey Lolich is the guy who won three games in the World Series of 1968. Tiger Stadium's center-field fence was always 440 feet away (even though it wasn't). Sparky Anderson is always the guy who promised he'd win a World Series in five years (and then did).

Tiger fans remember their history, and they remember their heroes.

And they remember the numbers that go along with them.

Detroit's

4

World Championships

Being a Tigers fan has always required patience. But being a Tigers fan has also meant that patience will be rewarded.

Each generation gets a championship moment—but just one. Each generation gets a set of heroes, but they move on before the next group can arrive.

Cobb gave way to Gehringer and Greenberg, who gave way to Newhouser, who gave way to Kaline, who gave way to Tram and Lou, who gave way to Verlander and Cabrera.

There were some gaps, but never long enough for anyone to start talking about a curse. Wait a few years, and the next group comes along. The next moment arrives.

Each generation ends up with a championship season to call its own.

In his fascinating book, *Baseball: The Fans' Game,* Mickey Cochrane wrote that 1935 was and would always be the high point of Tigers history.

"There will be other World Series, of course, and other hysterical celebrations," Cochrane wrote. "But for sheer high glee and generosity I do not believe the '35 triumph of the Detroit Tigers will ever be duplicated."

Care to disagree?

If you grew up with the 1984 Tigers, you probably do. Or with the 1968 Tigers. Or maybe even with the 1945 Tigers.

TIGER WORLD SERIES TEAMS

The Tigers don't top the list when it comes to World Series championships, but they're not at the bottom, either. Their four titles rank ninth among the 30 major-league organizations, and fourth among American League teams, behind only the Yankees (27), the A's (9) and the Red Sox (8).

The Tigers have been to the World Series 11 times:

1907 — lost 4–0 to Chicago Cubs

1908 — lost 4–1 to Chicago Cubs

1909 — lost 4–3 to Pittsburgh Pirates

1934 — lost 4–3 to St. Louis Cardinals

1935 — beat Chicago Cubs 4–2

1940 — lost 4–3 to Cincinnati Reds

1945 — beat Chicago Cubs 4–3

1968 — beat St. Louis Cardinals 4–3

1984 — beat San Diego Padres 4–1

2006 — lost 4–1 to St. Louis Cardinals

2012 — lost 4–0 to San Francisco Giants

The seasons to remember are spaced just right, so one doesn't blend in with another. The wait from one magical season to the next can feel like eternity (ask Al Kaline, whose only World Series came in his 16th season), but with few exceptions there's a championship ring in there somewhere.

In all, 28 men have played 12 or more years for the Tigers. Of those, all but three made it to a World Series wearing a Tiger uniform.

The earliest group—the Cobb-era Tigers—never won the World Series, but they remain the only teams in franchise history to win three consecutive American League titles (1907–09).

The 24-year gap between 1909 and 1934 remains the longest in franchise history without a trip to the Series, and perhaps that's one reason why the championship the following season set off such a wild celebration. It didn't hurt that the city and country were just coming out of the Depression, which hit the city's automobile industry especially hard.

There was also the memory of that '34 Series, when the Tigers came home from St. Louis with a three games to two lead but watched the Cardinals win two straight to take the title.

The themes would return with the championships to come, which helped the city celebrate after difficult times, and/or followed a near-miss season.

The '45 championship arrived just a month after the end of World War II. The '68 title helped Detroit recover from the devastation of the 1967 riots. The '84 title came at a time when the Detroit auto industry was really beginning to suffer.

The 1967 team lost the AL title on the final day of the season, and went home feeling it should have won. The 1983 Tigers finished second to the Orioles in the AL East, close enough to understand what it meant not to win.

"There wasn't a doubt in anyone's mind that we were the best team in the league when that season ended," Lance Parrish would say later. "We just ran out of games before we could get there."

Even the 2006 team, which didn't win the World Series, gave the franchise and its fans a sense of recovery. Nine of the 25 players on the World Series roster had also been part of the 2003 team that had to win five of its last six games simply to avoid a 120-loss season. Three other 2003 Tigers played a part in the 2006 season and earned World Series rings.

That group of Tigers is still trying to win a World Series title of its own, and trying to win one for owner Mike Ilitch the way the '84 team was able to hand a trophy to Tom Monaghan, and the '68 team was able to deliver for John Fetzer, the '45 team for Walter Briggs, and the '35 team for Frank Navin.

Even Tiger owners, it seems, all get to enjoy a year of glory if they wait long enough.

But rarely does anyone, be it owner, manager, player or fan, have more than one Tiger championship to call his own.

The 1935 team finished second to the Yankees the next two seasons. One player from that team, pitcher Elden Auker, wrote years later that "we would have won more than just the one World Series if Mr. Briggs had left Cochrane alone to run the team."

The 1968 Tigers followed their title with 90 wins, but the Orioles won 109 that year. The '84 Tigers would win 98 games three years later, but then lost in the playoffs to an 85-win Twins team.

Cochrane was player/manager in 1935, but Briggs fired him late in the 1938 season. The relatively unheralded Steve O'Neill managed the 1945 champions, and the even less heralded Mayo Smith was the manager in 1968. Sparky Anderson won his Tiger title in '84, and now Brad Ausmus is trying to win his.

Tiger history tells you there will be another one, probably not too far into the future. Tiger history tells you that every generation eventually gets its reward.

This generation is still waiting.

Al Kaline's

62

Years As a Tiger

The Tigers have been blessed with stars for every era. If one generation had Ty Cobb, the next had Gehringer and Greenberg. If one generation had Tram and Lou, the next had JV and Miggy.

But there's only one Al Kaline.

There's only one man so heavily associated with this franchise— and so fully committed to it—that he could have the title of Mr. Tiger.

Cobb played his final two seasons in Philadelphia with the Athletics. Gehringer went into business when his playing days were done. Greenberg became the general manager of the Cleveland Indians and later the Chicago White Sox. Trammell went off to coach with the San Diego Padres, and then on Kirk Gibson's staff with the Arizona Diamondbacks. Miguel Cabrera began his career as a Florida Marlin.

Kaline was a Tiger from the day he graduated high school in 1953. He's still a Tiger today.

He never played for another team. He never worked for another team. He even stayed on, well after the time he had planned to retire.

He had gone from player to broadcaster to trusted advisor, and he thought 50 years with one team sounded about right. But then when he got to 50, Kaline decided he wasn't done yet.

More than a decade later, he's still there, as trusted as ever, as respected as ever, as loyal as ever.

Maybe there's another man with another team in another sport who can match Kaline's 62 years (and counting) with the Tigers, but good luck finding him.

Good luck finding anyone who has had a life like Al Kaline's life.

"I hate to think about those people who have to go to work every day who really regret going to work," Kaline told biographer Jim Hawkins in his 2010 book. "There I was, at 18 years old, doing exactly what I wanted to do with my life. And I'm still doing exactly what I've wanted to do, ever since I was 13 years of age.

"How lucky can you be?"

It's more than luck, of course.

Kaline got the chance to sign with the Tigers at 18 because he was that good. He got the chance to play for the Tigers for 22 years because he was that good. He got the chance to become a Tiger broadcaster when he retired, because he was that loved. He got the chance to be a Tiger executive when he was done broadcasting, because he was that respected.

He still is.

The Tigers keep a locker for Kaline in their Comerica Park clubhouse, and players who were born 20 years after he last played a game understand who he is and why he's there. For years, Kaline has put on a uniform in spring training, working with Tiger outfielders.

KALINE'S TIGER RECORDS

Most games played ▸ **2,834**

Most seasons played: ▸ **22**
(tied with Ty Cobb)

Most home runs, career ▸ **399**

Most walks, career ▸ **1,277**

Most Gold Gloves ▸ **10**

Most All-Star appearances ▸ **18**

For years after he retired, he looked like he could still play.

He never thought he would stay so long. Sometime around 2002, just after he left the broadcast booth and was approaching 50 years with the Tigers, Kaline told me that he had always thought 50 would be a good place to stop, a nice round number. But he said then that he wasn't ready to stop, that he was enjoying his new role as front office advisor too much, that as long as his health kept up and his wife Louise didn't mind, he was going to keep working.

A few months later, I ran into Kaline at Detroit Metro Airport. We were both headed to the baseball winter meetings. He said it would be the first time he had ever been.

He boarded the plane with the other Tiger executives, and he took his seat—in coach. Al Kaline is a proud man, and rightfully so, but he's not someone who puts himself above everyone else.

Anyone who has spent time around the Tigers for the last half century has known him. Everyone who has spent time around the Tigers has liked him, and respected him.

His name remains in the Tiger record book, everywhere you look.

Only Cobb had more hits, drove in more runs, and had more total bases. Only Cobb and Charlie Gehringer scored more runs.

For years, Kaline also drew the Tigers' highest salary, and famously turned down a raise to $100,000 in 1971. Kaline had signed for $96,000, the same salary he made in 1970, and when general manager Jim Campbell called him in and said he wanted to make it $100,000, Kaline said no.

> *Maybe there's another man ... **who can match Kaline's 62 years** (and counting) **with the Tigers, but good luck finding him.***

"No, we have a contract," Kaline told Campbell. "I'll live up to that. I'll have a better year next year. If you want to give me $100,000 then, that'll be fine."

Kaline did live up to it, making the All-Star team for the first time since 1967. And the next year he did get $100,000.

"I never would have asked for it," Kaline told Hawkins years later. "But Jim Campbell said Mr. Fetzer wanted me to have it."

Kaline never could have guessed that he'd one day be in discussions about whether to acquire players making $20 million a year. Then again, when he signed his original contract with the Tigers for a $15,000 bonus (plus two years' salary at $6,000 a year), he could never have imagined that he'd someday have a $100,000 contract.

He could never have imagined that 62 years later, he'd still be going to work for the only team he has ever known, really the only employer he had ever known.

How lucky can you be?

Hughie Jennings Wins

3

Straight AL Pennants

Hughie Jennings would have been fun to watch.

You don't usually say that about a manager, but there haven't been many managers in baseball history like Hughie Jennings. The Tigers have had high-profile managers through their history—from Mickey Cochrane to Billy Martin to Sparky Anderson to Alan Trammell to Jim Leyland and now Brad Ausmus—but it's safe to say they've never had another manager like Jennings.

They've never had another manager take them to three straight World Series, either. For that matter, they've never had another manager take them to three World Series, consecutive or otherwise.

All while yelling "Eee-yahhhh!" or "Wee-ah!" or "Eee-ya!" or whatever it was that Jennings famously yelled while coaching third base. And while kicking his left leg in the air.

Imagine Sparky or Leyland trying to do that.

Jennings was a coal miner as a kid, and a lawyer later in life. He was known as the best shortstop of his day ("No one compared with Hughie," Honus Wagner once said), and also known for leading the league five straight years in getting hit by pitches (although he seemed to rarely miss a game because of it).

Jennings would later say that his father liked it better when he worked as a mule driver in the coal mines.

"Mules did not drink, and my father had heard that ballplayers did," Jennings told the *New York Evening World.*

... the Tigers had
5 managers in
first 6 seasons
in the American League.

He still chose baseball, and he took over as the Tigers manager when he was just 38 years old. Owner Frank Navin paid $1,000 to draft him from the minor-league Baltimore Orioles as a player in September 1906, even though by that time Jennings was no longer playing regularly and even though he would never play regularly in Detroit (he appeared in six games over five seasons, most on days after the Tigers had clinched the pennant).

The Tigers had gone through five managers in their first six seasons in the American League, and had never finished higher than third place. They already had a pair of Hall of Famers in the lineup: young Ty Cobb, who had yet to develop into being baseball's best player, and Wahoo Sam Crawford, already in his prime.

Jennings predicted a pennant before his Tigers ever played a game, but his first Tiger team didn't start fast. The Tigers spent most of the season in third place, and didn't take over first place for good until the final two weeks.

When they clinched their first-ever pennant, with an October 5 win in St. Louis, the Detroit City Council declared a holiday, and stores put photos of Jennings in their windows.

"Jennings is now the reigning star of the baseball world," the *Detroit News* wrote.

MOST PENNANTS WON, TIGER MANAGERS

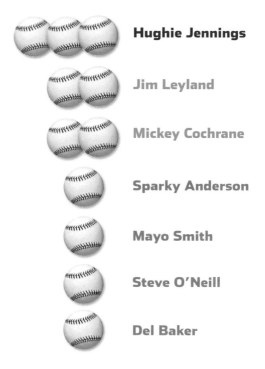

Hughie Jennings

Jim Leyland

Mickey Cochrane

Sparky Anderson

Mayo Smith

Steve O'Neill

Del Baker

Tiger fans had quickly taken to the new manager. They took to imitating his "Eee-yahhhh!" yell. Jennings never fully explained what he was saying or why, although he did claim to have coined the phrase "Atta-boy!"

It wasn't just the yells. Jennings would dance, he would whistle, he would pick the grass and throw it in the air. He was a show in himself, and the Tigers became the best road draw in the league, and in 1909 became the first AL team to play before 1 million fans (home and road combined).

Not everyone enjoyed the show. AL president Ban Johnson suspended Jennings for using a tin whistle. A writer called Jennings "silly, destructive, and an insult to American League fans." But Jennings kept right on with the show, even picking up a rubber snake and a jack-in-the-box to distract Philadelphia Athletics pitcher Rube Waddell.

Jennings was more than just a clown, though. He had been a great player, and he knew the game. Soon after taking over the Tigers, he took one look at Cobb and said: "Hear me? This boy [Cobb] has it. He has the makings to become the greatest player who ever lived."

Jennings did get frustrated with Cobb's racism and his tendency to get in trouble, and briefly tried to trade him away. But Jennings and Cobb would remain together and would work together, and the two of them would lead the first great era of Tiger baseball.

1907 ▶ **92-58**

1908 ▶ **90-63**

1909 ▶ **98-54**

"He helped me become a pretty good ballplayer simply by letting me play my own way," Cobb wrote years later.

Cobb didn't need to follow Jennings' signs. He didn't need to show up at morning practices. He rarely got to the ballpark before 2:00 PM, in an era when all games were played in the afternoon. There were days he didn't even make first pitch, and the Tigers would start another player in center field and allow Cobb to enter the game whenever he showed up.

Jennings put up with it, and Cobb did become the greatest player of his era, quite possibly the greatest who ever lived. Cobb was a .375 hitter in Jennings' 14 seasons, with a .962 OPS and a 185 OPS-plus, which suggests he was 85 percent above league average for those years.

The one thing Cobb and Jennings never did together was win a World Series. The Tigers lost to the Chicago Cubs in 1907 and 1908, and to the Pittsburgh Pirates in 1909. And despite keeping their best players together, they never got back.

They came close a couple of times, most notably in 1915, when the Tigers won 100 games (more than in any of the pennant seasons) but the Boston Red Sox won 101. Jennings would call that season "my biggest disappointment in Detroit," but the Tigers did well enough that Navin gave his manager a new contract.

He got five more years, but the Tigers didn't get another pennant, and wouldn't until 1934. By 1920, Jennings had lost much of what made him so popular, and when that season ended, he announced he was retiring to go back to Scranton, Pennsylvania, and practice law.

Cobb would take over the Tigers as player/manager. Jennings would go to New York to work with his old teammate John McGraw (where he helped the Giants win two World Series). But the standards they set in Detroit wouldn't soon be forgotten.

Cobb was a .375 hitter in Jennings' 14 seasons, with a .962 OPS and a 185 OPS-plus.

Jennings won 1,131 games in his 14 seasons with the Tigers, a number that would be topped by Sparky Anderson more than 70 years later. He won three American League pennants, a record that still hasn't been matched in Detroit, a full century later.

Sparky was a character, without doubt, sometimes as much fun to watch as his many fine teams. But has there ever been a more fun manager, with the Tigers or any other team, than Hughie Jennings?

Ty Cobb's Lifetime

.367*

Batting Average

Rooting for the Ty Cobb Tigers had to be a little like cheering for the Barry Bonds Giants.

You were watching the best player you'd ever seen. You'd argue he was the best player anyone had ever seen.

And everyone else hated him.

Bonds remains in the record books as baseball's all-time home run leader, even if many refuse to recognize it. Cobb remains in the record book as baseball's best hitter for average, even if many would just as soon drop that stat from its traditional spot as baseball's most-quoted number.

Bonds was so sure he was the best that it pained him when players like Mark McGwire and Sammy Sosa got more attention. In the book *Game of Shadows,* authors Mark Fainaru-Wada and Lance Williams say that pain led him to use steroids.

Cobb was so sure he was the best that it pained him when Babe Ruth started getting more attention for his home runs. Steroids weren't available to Cobb, but given how he was willing to do anything to win, don't you think he might have tried them if he could have?

Let's not take the comparison too far—Tiger fans might say we have already, as no one is calling for Cobb's record to be taken away. Cobb's actual career batting average has been argued over the years (baseball still lists it at .367, while baseball-reference. com goes with .366), but it's always been considered legitimate.

Cobb was hated. In many ways, he was despicable, on and off the field.

TY COBB'S HIGHEST BATTING AVERAGES

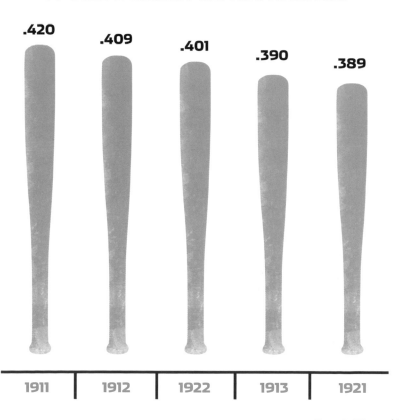

.420 .409 .401 .390 .389

| 1911 | 1912 | 1922 | 1913 | 1921 |

Cobb sharing a rare smile.
(New York Times/ Getty Images)

But he sure could play. Wouldn't you have loved to have the chance to see him, even for just one game?

Cobb arrived in Detroit direct from Augusta of the South Atlantic League, an 18-year-old called on as an August fill-in because the 1905 Tigers had some injuries. He had never been to the North. He had never been to a big city. And he had just buried his beloved father, who was shot by his mother in suspicious circumstances.

He doubled in a run on his first at-bat, against New York's Jack Chesbro, who walked him the next time up.

He quickly developed a reputation for being hated by all, including his teammates. He also quickly developed a reputation for doing anything to win, and soon developed a reputation for being the best hitter in the game.

He hit .366 or .367 over a career of 3,034 or 3,035 games. He had 4,191 hits, a record that stood until Pete Rose topped it, and still stands as the most in American League history (although baseball-reference.com now credits Cobb with only 4,189). Rickey Henderson took away his record for all-time runs scored.

Cobb overtook Nap Lajoie for the career batting average record in 1911. More than 100 years have passed (and many of Cobb's other records have fallen), but no one has overtaken Cobb on the career average list.

There's a pretty good chance no one will anytime soon, either. Miguel Cabrera's .320 career average is the best among active players. Even if Cabrera hit safely in his next 450 at-bats, he still wouldn't catch Cobb.

Cabrera has hit .300 or better each of the last six years, a remarkable streak in today's game (tied with Robinson Cano for the longest active streak). Cobb hit .300 or better in each of his last 23 seasons in the majors.

Cobb also hit .400 three times, including in back-to-back seasons. He won 11 batting titles, and he was a good enough teacher of hitting that Tiger players won five more batting crowns after Cobb became player/manager in 1921.

Don't trust batting average as a stat? That's fine. Cobb led the American League in oWAR (offensive wins above replacement) eight times. He owns the top five seasons in offensive WAR in Tiger history, and also the top five seasons in total WAR.

Cobb held 43 different major league records when he retired, although it's worth noting that the modern major leagues came to be just a few seasons before his debut. Even all those numbers didn't tell the whole story, because Cobb was also famous for how often he would take an extra base or intimidate an opponent into a mistake.

"He didn't outhit and he didn't outrun them," longtime teammate (and antagonist) Sam Crawford said. "He outthought them."

By any measure, he was the best player of his era, perhaps the best of any era. When it came time to elect the initial class for the Hall of Fame, Cobb received 222 of a possible 226 votes, easily more than any other player.

Two years after Cobb died, in 1961, the Tigers unveiled a plaque that hung outside their Tiger Stadium offices and now hangs outside the offices at Comerica Park.

"Tyrus Raymond Cobb, 1886–1961," it reads. "Greatest Tiger of All. A Genius in Spikes."

He was all of that, and Detroit fans loved him for it. But he was also "Tyrus the Terrible," as biographer Al Stump referred to him in a 1985 article about Cobb's final days. He was also so hated around the country that all of baseball was said to be cheering for Honus Wagner's 1909 Pittsburgh Pirates to beat Cobb's Tigers in the World Series (which they did).

Cobb was so hated by his teammates that the Tigers tried hard to trade him after the 1906 season, and so disliked around the league that they couldn't find a taker. Even years later, he was still so hated that he was thwarted in his attempts to buy a team, despite having enough money (or partners with money) to do it.

Crawford said Cobb was "still fighting the Civil War," which ended only 40 years before he left Georgia to head north and join the Tigers. But there was more to him than that.

He'd sharpen his spikes, and he'd sharpen his tongue.

Cobb was fascinating, a millionaire player before his time because of his investments in Coca-Cola and other companies, as well as a later-in-life hunting buddy of Ernest Hemingway.

But even Hemingway once described Cobb by saying, "He had a screw loose.... It was like his brain was miswired so that the least damned thing would set him off."

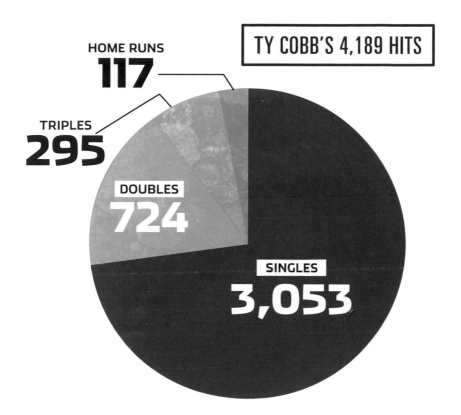

HOME RUNS
117

TRIPLES
295

TY COBB'S 4,189 HITS

DOUBLES
724

SINGLES
3,053

It's easy to say you'd have hated him, except for one thing. He could really play the game, and he really did help his teams win. The Tigers were also-rans in the first years of the American League, and it was the decision to buy Cobb from the Augusta team for $750 that played the biggest part in making them three-time AL champions.

Cobb's Tigers never won a World Series, just as Bonds' Giants never did. But for Tiger fans of the early 20th century, what he did was more than enough.

Tram and Lou Play

1,918

Games Together

There was a time, early in the 1995 season, when the marketing people decided the Tigers really needed an alternate home uniform. Other teams were doing it and making money on it, and the Tigers were going to do it, too.

And on a Sunday morning, they showed up in their Tiger Stadium clubhouse and found dark blue jerseys and white pinstriped pants.

"I feel like a Yankee," Lou Whitaker said as he pulled on the pinstripes, not enjoying the thought.

The Tigers never wore those uniforms. An hour or so before game time, club president John McHale went to the clubhouse and vetoed the idea. The Tigers would wear their traditional home whites, as they have for every home game since (save for a few Negro League tribute games).

Lou could feel like a Tiger, all through his 2,390-game major league career. For almost all of those games, and for all 19 of his major league seasons, he could look to his right and see Alan Trammell feeling like a Tiger, too.

Both had chances to leave. Neither one ever did, at least not until their playing careers ended.

Other teammates with other teams have stayed together as long or even longer (although the 1,918 games Trammell and Whitaker played together remain an American League record). Others have had their names forever linked, as Tiger fans link Tram and Lou. But no one else has done what Tram and Lou did, arriving on the same day and serving as a double-play combination for basically the next two decades.

They played second base and shortstop. They batted 1-2 in the Tiger lineup in a World Series. They wore No. 1 and No. 3, and though the numbers haven't been retired (Gary Sheffield wore No. 3 in his time as a Tiger and Ian Kinsler is wearing it now, and Jose Iglesias is wearing No. 1), you would think that someday they will be.

It's a shame they couldn't have gone into the Hall of Fame as a tandem. It's a shame that neither may make the Hall on his own.

"Tram and I will get there," Whitaker said, when the 1984 Tigers gathered in 2014 for their 30-year reunion. "Everybody is rushing. You don't rush greatness. We'll wait. We'll wait. That day will come.

"We know we deserve to be in there. We know how good we were."

We knew how good they were, almost right from the start.

They were drafted a year apart, Whitaker in 1975 out of Martinsville High in Virginia, Trammell in 1976 out of Kearny High in San Diego. They retired a year apart, too, with Trammell deciding to hang on through the 1996 season after Whitaker retired at the end of 1995.

Amazingly, they finished with almost the exact same number of career hits, with Whitaker just four hits ahead of Trammell at 2,369 to 2,365. They had a similar career OPS (.789 for Whitaker, .767 for Trammell), and a similar career WAR (74.9 for Whitaker, 70.4 for Trammell).

They weren't together all the time, but they were together on the field and they'll always be together in our minds.

"We weren't close friends," Trammell would say years later. "It wasn't like that. But there was this communication that we developed. We were inside each other's head."

Trammell was drafted as a shortstop and never played anywhere else until late in his career (when he played third base, second base, and even the outfield). Whitaker was drafted as a third baseman and didn't move to second until the fall instructional league after the 1976 season, when he and Trammell first became a double-play pairing at the suggestion of general manager Jim Campbell.

...played together in

October 1995

for the final time.

"Whitaker is such a natural athlete that he took to second base right away," Tigers infield instructor Ed Brinkman said then.

Campbell acted against the objections of farm director Hoot Evers, who wanted to leave Whitaker at third base. No one, though, was disputing the idea that Trammell and Whitaker could be the core of the Tigers' bright future.

When Bill Lajoie had his scouts together in Florida during that 1976 instructional league, he told them to shake hands with the two youngsters.

"Because those are the kinds of young men I want you to be looking for," said Lajoie, then the Tigers' scouting director.

Trammell and Whitaker were together in 1977 at Double-A Montgomery, where they played for Brinkman on a team that won the Southern League championship. They would come to the major leagues that September, debuting together in the second game of a doubleheader at Fenway Park. Tram and Lou combined for five hits, but a Tiger team finishing off a sub-.500 season lost to the Red Sox 8–6.

By the next spring, they were regulars. Whitaker was the American League's Rookie of the Year. Trammell finished fourth.

By 1983, they would both get MVP votes. In 1984, they were both All-Stars—and world champions.

And two decades later, when Trammell came back to the Tigers as manager, Whitaker took part in spring training as an instructor.

They were back together, and back in the only uniform they ever wore as players, through a combined 4,683 games. There were times they could have gone elsewhere, times when it seemed that they would. Whitaker was courted as a free agent by the Braves, Orioles, and Yankees. Late in his career, Trammell was often mentioned as a possible pennant-race addition, perhaps even by his hometown Padres.

There was also the one spring training, in 1985, when manager Sparky Anderson wanted to move Whitaker to third base to make room for rookie Chris Pittaro. The announcement got plenty of attention, but the plan didn't last more than a few days.

Eight years later, Sparky would make another switch, moving Trammell to third base for a month and playing Travis Fryman at shortstop. Soon enough, though, he changed his mind and reunited Tram and Lou.

They played together for the last time on the first day of October, 1995, the final day of that season and Anderson's final game as manager. Sparky had them play one inning, then sent Steve Rodriguez (at second base) and Chris Gomez (at shortstop) out to replace them.

In the 19 years since, the Tigers have opened the season with 15 different double-play combinations. In all, they've used 38 different starting second basemen since Whitaker retired, and 27 different starting shortstops since Trammell.

That's not really unusual. What's unusual—unheard of, really—is for two guys to last side-by-side the way Trammell and Whitaker did.

Tigers Start

35–5

in 1984

This is a book about the Tigers, and a book about numbers, and there's one number that will never be forgotten.

Two numbers, actually. Separated by a hyphen.

35–5.

You really don't need to say anything more. There's no number more associated with any Tiger team, perhaps with any team.

35–5.

Thirty years on, it's still incredible that it happened. Thirty years on, no team has even come close to matching it.

And 30 years on, when you think back to a 1984 season that remains a magical memory, 35–5 might well be the first thing that comes to mind.

There's no doubt it's the first number that comes to mind from that season. A whole lot more people can tell you that the Tigers started 35–5 than could remember that they finished 104–58, or even that they swept the Kansas City Royals in the playoffs or that they clinched the World Series with an 8–4 win in Game 5.

Or that Willie Hernandez had 32 saves, or that Jack Morris had 19 wins, or that Alan Trammell hit .314, and Lance Parrish hit 33 home runs. Or that Kirk Gibson had the first of his four 20–20 seasons, the first 20-homer, 20-steal season in Tiger history.

Only six teams in the history of baseball have ever won 35 of 40 at any point in a season.

The Tigers did so many things well that year, and provided so many memorable moments. But they were never more dominating, never more impressive and never more unprecedented than they were in those incredible first 40 games.

Nobody starts a season 35–5. Only six teams in the history of baseball have ever won 35 of 40 at any point in a season. It's only happened twice in the last 78 years (the Royals did it late in the 1977 season), only three times in the last 100 years (the New York Giants did it midway through the 1936 season).

The New York Yankees, for all their history and their 27 World Series titles, have never done 35–5—not to start a season, not to end a season, and not at any point in between.

No, when you say 35–5, every baseball fan anywhere says '84 Tigers. It really is that special.

And it really was that incredible, even if the Tigers came out of Lakeland that spring believing they were headed for a special season. As they broke camp, manager Sparky Anderson told his friend and PR man Dan Ewald, "I got a feeling. Something tremendous is gonna happen."

Even Sparky couldn't have predicted what did happen.

The Tigers had a no-hitter (by Jack Morris in Chicago) before they had a loss. They had three walk-off wins before they had two losses. They had two nine-game winning streaks and two seven-game winning streaks before they ever had a three-game losing streak.

They won their first 17 road games. Nineteen years later, in that horrible 2003 season, the Tigers would only win 20 road games all year.

The Tigers had

1 no-hitter

before their first loss.

"They were better than everybody every night," said Rod Allen, who had a front-row seat as a rookie bench player on that team. "It wasn't luck."

Trammell had 54 hits, 36 runs, and a .958 OPS during that 40-game stretch. Lou Whitaker had 52 hits and scored 31 runs. Parrish and Chet Lemon had seven home runs apiece, and Lemon drove in 32 runs.

Morris was 9–1, with a 1.97 ERA, and Dan Petry was 7–1, with a 2.81. Aurelio Lopez had four wins and a 1.47 ERA out of the bullpen, and Hernandez already had seven saves.

He would have had more, but the Tigers outscored their opponents 236–120. In 12 of the 35 wins, they took the lead in the first inning and never gave it up. In 11 other games, they were ahead for good by the third inning.

When they swept the Angels in Anaheim on the next-to-last weekend of May to go to 35–5, the Tigers held an 8½-game lead over the second-place Toronto Blue Jays. The Jays actually held the second-best record in baseball at that point, a record that would have given them the division lead a year later.

Sparky worried that there were still 122 games to play, plenty of time for the Blue Jays to make up 8½ games. He worried about everything, worried so much that he would say years later that

1984 was actually one of the most stressful years of his managerial career.

"When you start 35–5, you have to win," he wrote in *They Call Me Sparky.* "Every time a visiting manager came to Detroit after that, I told them to take a look at that flagpole in center field. If we don't win, there's only gonna be one person hanging from it. It ain't gonna be no players. It's ain't gonna be no coaches. It ain't gonna be the general manager and it sure ain't gonna be the owner.

"The only person hanging from that pole if we didn't win was gonna be little ol' Sparky.... I couldn't shake that feeling all season long."

They did win, of course. They didn't have the best record in the league from that point on, but they came close, going 69–53 (half a game worse than the New York Yankees). The Blue Jays would creep to within 3½ games for one day in early June, but the Tigers would win the division going away, with a 15-game cushion.

And the only thing hanging from that flagpole, beneath the American flag, was the flag celebrating Detroit's fourth world championship.

Jim Leyland's

5

Playoffs in Eight Years

A week or so before the Tigers hired Jim Leyland as their 36th manager, I was talking with someone in the organization about how much difference a good manager would really make.

"I guess we're about to find out," was the answer.

I guess we did.

It's not fair to blame the five managers between Sparky Anderson and Jim Leyland for the Tigers' long playoff drought. But it sure is fair to give Leyland a good share of the credit for ending the drought and beginning the most consistent stretch of October baseball in franchise history.

Yes, Leyland came to the Tigers at the right time, when some young talent was ready to shine and when Mike Ilitch's wallet had started to open. But you could just as easily say that the Tigers hired Leyland at the right time, when a first-rate manager really could make a difference.

JIM LEYLAND'S RECORD AS TIGER MANAGER

= WINS = LOSSES

700 WINS

597 LOSSES

2006: 95–67***

2009: 86–77*

2011: 95–67**

2012: 88–74***

2013: 93–69**

*lost Game 163 to Twins

**advanced to ALCS

***advanced to World Series

Maybe that was still hard to see on October 3, 2005, two days after the Tigers finished their 12th straight losing season and their 18th straight playoff-less season. Alan Trammell's Tigers lost an amazing 300 games in three years, and if there was any sign of improvement, it was minimal.

Leyland drove from Pittsburgh to Detroit that day. He convinced his old boss Dave Dombrowski that he still had the fire that helped the two of them win a World Series in Florida. Leyland was introduced at Comerica Park the next day—"[This] is a very big day for our franchise," Dombrowski said—and a year later, Comerica was rocking as the Tigers eliminated the heavily favored New York Yankees in the Division Series.

Seven days later, Magglio Ordonez hit the home run that will long be remembered, the one that sent the Tigers to their first World Series in 22 years.

Leyland would take the Tigers back to the World Series six years later, becoming just the third manager in franchise history to make it to the Series more than once (Hughie Jennings and Mickey Cochrane are the other two). He would get to four American League Championship Series, and have one other season end in a classic single-game tie-breaking playoff loss to the Minnesota Twins.

Baseball refers to that 2009 meeting with the Twins as "Game 163," and not as an official playoff appearance, but it sure did feel like a playoff game.

Tigers lost an amazing

300 games

in three years ...

By the time Leyland retired at the end of the 2013 ALCS, his Tiger teams were a combined 103 games over .500. Only Jennings, who managed the Ty Cobb–led Tigers for 14 seasons (and to three World Series) in the early days of the 20th century, was further over .500 as a Tiger manager.

Leyland, who began his baseball career as a Tiger minor leaguer and then as a minor-league manager, proved the Tigers right for their decision to bring him back—and perhaps proved them wrong for their decision to let him go in the first place.

He never wanted to leave, but by 1981 Leyland had already spent 10 seasons managing in the Tiger farm system. He had already spent three years at Triple-A. The Tigers had hired Sparky Anderson three years before, and Sparky wasn't leaving anytime soon.

Tony La Russa, who would become one of Leyland's closest friends, was then named manager of the Chicago White Sox. He wanted Leyland as his third-base coach.

Leyland told Bill Lajoie that even if all the Tigers could offer was a job as the bullpen coach on the big-league staff, he would take that over the more prestigious third-base coaching job with La Russa. But Sparky had his own people, and Sparky said no.

Leyland would always say that he understood, but he would also always say that one of the hardest things he ever had to do was to tell his mother that he was leaving the Tigers.

As it turned out, the move worked out for him. Four seasons with the White Sox led to a big-league managing job with the Pittsburgh Pirates, and eventually to three straight playoff appearances. The job with the Pirates led to the Marlins and Dombrowski and a World Series ring, and eventually back to the Tigers.

... Leyland retired at the end of the 2013 ALCS, his Tiger teams were a combined 103 games over .500.

Dombrowski came to Detroit as club president after the 2001 season. He inherited manager Phil Garner, and went through Luis Pujols and then Trammell without ever having anything close to a winning season.

He knew he needed a new manager, and perhaps he knew what difference a good manager could make (although no, he wasn't the person I talked to that day).

Jim Leyland did make a difference. Five playoff appearances in eight years (even if one was only a Game 163) will tell you that.

Justin Verlander's

2

No-Hitters

It seems crazy to say this, but there was never a question that Justin Verlander was going to throw a no-hitter. And when he threw one, there was never a question that there would be another one.

Pitchers go to the Hall of Fame without ever throwing a no-hitter. Before Verlander, only one pitcher in Tiger history (Virgil Trucks) had thrown more than one, and that was 60 years ago.

And yet, somehow we all knew Verlander was going to do it. From almost the first day he put on a Tiger uniform, somehow we all knew he was different.

He could throw his fastball 100 mph. His curveball could be unhittable, but you had to swing at it, because he'd throw it for a strike. The changeup was sick, as pitchers and hitters say.

By the middle of his second full year in the big leagues, I'd written a column for Booth Newspapers suggesting that Verlander might strike out 20 batters in a game. Instead, that night at Comerica Park against the Milwaukee Brewers, he threw a no-hitter.

Okay, so I was wrong, but what a night that was.

"It was," Brandon Inge said then, "one of the coolest things ever."

It was, except that the guy in the spotlight was hardly cool. In fact, if you ask Justin Verlander now to describe his two no-hitters, what sticks out about that first one is how he couldn't calm himself down.

"I was standing on the mound in the ninth thinking, 'Do I really belong here? Do I deserve to throw a no-hitter in the big leagues when I'd never thrown one anywhere?'" Verlander said, seven years later. "I remember pure adrenaline running through my body, trying to get myself calm and not being able to."

There were games early in Verlander's career where those emotions would get the best of him, where he got moving so fast that he couldn't slow down, so fast that he would lose control of himself and the game. But there were also games where you could tell early on that he was going to dominate, where it seemed that the hitters just didn't have a chance.

He could throw his fastball

100 MPH.

"It just didn't matter that night," he said. "My stuff was so good. I was throwing 86, 87 mph curves that looked like a fastball until the last minute. That game and the game before in Texas, those two games back-to-back were probably the best stuff I've ever had."

Verlander had already been the American League Rookie of the Year, had already helped pitch the Tigers to their first World Series appearance in 22 years. The Tigers' brutal 2003 season had earned them the second overall pick in the 2004 draft (the top pick alternated between the two leagues back then), and scouting director Greg Smith's decision to take Verlander turned out to be one of the key moments in the turnaround of the Tiger franchise.

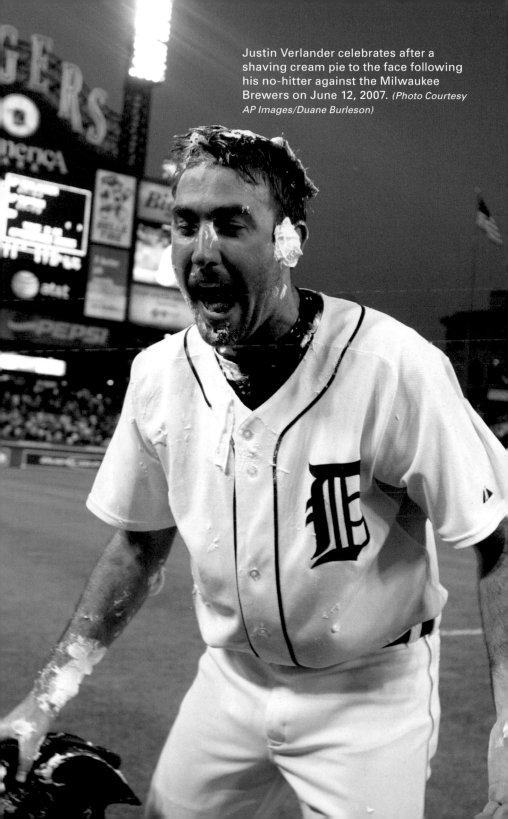

Justin Verlander celebrates after a shaving cream pie to the face following his no-hitter against the Milwaukee Brewers on June 12, 2007. *(Photo Courtesy AP Images/Duane Burleson)*

The no-hitter against the Brewers only seemed to confirm that. The Tigers hadn't had a pitcher throw a no-hitter since Jack Morris did it in Chicago in the first week of the 1984 season; no Tiger had thrown a no-hitter in Detroit since Trucks in May 1952.

Presumably, Trucks was pretty dominant in that game against the Washington Senators. But it's hard to believe he was as good as Verlander was in 2007 against the Brewers.

"This was the most dominating performance I've ever seen in my life," said Sean Casey, who played in a game where Randy Johnson struck out 20.

By 2009, Verlander would become a 19-game winner and the third-place finisher in AL Cy Young voting. By May 2011, when he took the mound for a Saturday afternoon game at Toronto's Rogers Centre, he was already considered one of the very best pitchers in the game.

Then he threw his second no-hitter.

It was really nothing like the first one, a point Verlander himself made in a later conversation.

"I remember a calming feeling," he said. "Everything I was doing was very methodical. That's not like me. And I think that translated into the post no-hitter celebration."

The first no-hitter ended with Magglio Ordonez making a catch just shy of the warning track in right field, as Verlander fired his arms into the air and almost flew into the embrace of catcher Pudge Rodriguez. The second no-hitter ended with Verlander striking out Rajai Davis, then giving two understated fist pumps and waiting at the mound for catcher Alex Avila.

Perhaps it would have been different if home-plate umpire Jerry Meals gave Verlander a borderline strike call at the end of J.P. Arencibia's 12-pitch at-bat with one out in the eighth inning. Meals said that the 100-mph fastball was just outside, and Arencibia's walk was the only thing that stood between Verlander and a perfect game.

"Right out of my fingertips, I knew it was just a hair outside, and it was," Verlander said that day. "It was a ball, and you've got to give [credit]—he called it a ball, and it was."

Verlander was that close to being perfect against the Blue Jays, and he wasn't far from perfect that season. He went 24–5 with a 2.40 ERA and 250 strikeouts, becoming the first Tiger since Hal Newhouser in 1945 to lead the league in all three categories.

He won the Cy Young Award, but was also named the Most Valuable Player, becoming the first starting pitcher to win both since Boston's Roger Clemens did it in 1986.

He went 24–5 with a 2.40 ERA and 250 strikeouts.

"That [no-hit] game turned a corner for me, and made me into the MVP and Cy Young pitcher that year," Verlander said.

And the only question remaining after that no-hitter was when (not if) Verlander was going to throw another one.

Miguel Cabrera Ends MLB's

45

Year Triple Crown Drought

The Triple Crown had become one of those things we talked about every few years but never actually believed we would see. Kind of like a .400 hitter or a 30-game winner—theoretically possible, but increasingly unlikely.

Then in 2012, Miguel Cabrera did it.

He jumped out to a big lead in home runs and RBIs, and held off late challenges from Curtis Granderson (in home runs) and Josh Hamilton (in both categories). He hit for a decent average in the first half of the season, then hit .344 in July and .357 in August. He still trailed Mike Trout by six points in the batting race with a month to go, but Cabrera hit .333 in September and Trout hit .289, and that was enough.

Cabrera was the American League batting champion for the second straight season. He was the home run champion for the second time, and the RBI champion for the second time.

Miguel Cabrera poses with Frank Robinson and Bud Selig as he receives the Triple Crown Award before Game 3 of the 2012 World Series. *(Photo Courtesy AP Photo/Paul Sancya)*

He was the first man since Carl Yastrzemski in 1967 to win all three in the same season.

"This is a huge story, and I want everybody to enjoy it," said manager Jim Leyland, who added to the drama by pulling Cabrera from the game in the middle of an inning in the Tigers' final game in Kansas City, after it was seemingly clear that he had clinched the Triple Crown.

The Tigers had only had one Triple Crown winner in their history, with Ty Cobb winning it in 1909 when it only took nine home runs to lead the league. Eleven other players before Cabrera had done it in baseball's modern era, and every one of them is a Hall of Famer.

"I tell everyone, we watch baseball history every day [with Cabrera]," Tiger broadcaster Jim Price likes to say. "I've never seen anything like it."

Few have.

In Cabrera's first six seasons with the Tigers, he hit .327 with 227 home runs and 737 RBIs. No one in the major leagues hit more home runs or drove in more runs in that span. Only Joe Mauer had Cabrera beat in batting average, and only by a single point.

Yes, Cabrera was that close to a six-year Triple Crown!

He was so good that when he won one Triple Crown—the first anyone had won in 45 years—his teammates were thinking he could do it again.

"I would not be shocked," Gerald Laird said the following spring.

Cabrera didn't win it again in 2013, but he did lead the American League in batting average and RBIs at the All-Star break. He did win a third straight batting title, while finishing second to Chris Davis in home runs (53–44) and RBIs (138–137). He came closer than anyone ever has to winning back-to-back Triple Crowns.

And he did win a second straight American League MVP Award.

Cabrera's 2012 MVP was much-discussed, because many fans who favor modern statistics believe the Triple Crown categories

MIGUEL CABRERA'S AL CROWNS

BATTING AVERAGE

2011 ┈┈▶ **.344**

2012 ┈┈▶ **.330**

2013 ┈┈▶ **.348**

HOME RUNS

2008 ┈┈▶ **37**

2012 ┈┈▶ **44**

RUNS BATTED IN

2010 ┈┈▶ **126**

2012 ┈┈▶ **139**

are less indicative of success than other stats. Many made the case for Mike Trout, who because of superior baserunning and defense led Cabrera in numbers like wins above replacement (WAR).

Many players, coaches, and managers wondered how there was even a debate. And when the Baseball Writers Association of

America released the voting totals, it wasn't even close. Cabrera took 22 of the 28 first-place votes, and led Trout by 81 points in overall voting.

Cabrera won the MVP by an even bigger margin in 2013, even without the Triple Crown. He became just the second back-to-back winner in Tiger history, the first since Hal Newhouser in 1944–45.

And he was still just 30 years old.

... he hit .327 with 227 home runs and 737 RBIs.

Cabrera was just 24 and already a star when the Tigers stunned the baseball world by acquiring him from the Marlins at the 2007 winter meetings. He had made it to the big leagues at age 20, so he was already just two years from free agency, and the Marlins knew they couldn't keep him.

The Tigers knew they could.

Before they left Lakeland to begin the 2008 season, they'd already agreed to an eight-year, $152.3 million contract. Two years before that deal was to end, the Tigers gave Cabrera a new eight-year deal, this one for $248 million.

The way he was producing, no one was arguing that it was too much money.

How much is a Triple Crown winner worth? Who could say, because the last one before Cabrera played in an era before free agency, an era when even $100,000 was a lot of money to pay a player?

For the record, the Red Sox gave Carl Yastrzemski $100,000 in 1968.

Yes, that was a long time ago.

Hal Newhouser's

2

MVP Awards

Hal Newhouser is still the only pitcher in baseball history to win back-to-back MVP Awards.

He's also the only pitcher to nearly win three in a row.

He won in 1944, and he won in 1945. And in 1946, he finished second—a fairly close second—behind Ted Williams.

Remember that the next time you hear someone refer to Newhouser as a "war-time player," someone who is somehow less worthy because he won while the real players were away fighting (or playing for Army baseball teams). Remember that when all the "real" players returned, Newhouser had a season that by some measures was actually his best.

Newhouser deserves his spot in baseball's Hall of Fame, and he didn't deserve the 38-year wait between retirement and enshrinement. He deserves his spot in Tiger history, and he deserves the statue that stands behind the left-center-field fence at Comerica Park, alongside those of Ty Cobb, Charlie Gehringer, Hank Greenberg, Willie Horton, and Al Kaline.

Oh, and he deserved the nickname "Prince Hal," even if he spent the early part of his career known as "Hurricane Hal" instead.

He was a little difficult early on. He had a bad temper, he didn't get along with teammates and he didn't get along with opponents. There were times it seemed the only answer for the Tigers was to trade him away, especially since his performance in the early days didn't make him seem worth the trouble.

Newhouser couldn't throw strikes (7.1 walks per nine innings as a 20-year-old in 1941), and he couldn't win (a 34–52 record through his first four big-league seasons). He wanted to join the Army Air Force, and even planned to be sworn in on the mound at Briggs Stadium, but a heart problem left him classified 4-F, unfit for duty.

His father found him an off-season job as an apprentice draftsman at Chrysler, and when Newhouser showed enough promise to be offered a full-time position, he thought about taking it. But he wanted to give baseball another shot. He wanted to try to make it with the Tigers, his hometown team, the team he had signed with for $4,000, even though the Cleveland Indians offered him $15,000.

He wanted to work with Steve O'Neill, who took over in 1943 as the Tigers manager, and with Paul Richards, the veteran catcher O'Neill brought in to work with his young pitchers.

"I'm going to make you a pitcher," Richards told Newhouser in the spring of 1944.

Richards taught Newhouser to throw a slider, and he taught him to control his emotions (although Newhouser later said he only controlled his temper because he started winning). Hurricane Hal turned into Prince Hal, and the kid who nearly quit the game became the game's best pitcher.

A year after leading the league in walks, Newhouser led the AL in strikeouts instead (while his walk total plummeted). The improved command allowed him to become a 300-inning pitcher, and a 29-game winner.

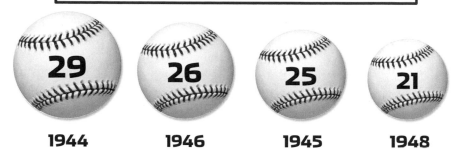

HAL NEWHOUSER'S WINNINGEST SEASONS

29	26	25	21
1944	1946	1945	1948

The Tigers won 88 games and finished a game out of first place, but Newhouser and rotation mate Dizzy Trout were the top two contenders for MVP. Trout had a lower ERA and more innings, but Newhouser had two more wins and all those strikeouts.

Trout received 10 first-place votes to Newhouser's seven, but when all the other votes were added up, Newhouser won one of the closest votes in MVP history.

A year later, as the war was ending and players began returning (Hank Greenberg rejoined the Tigers at midseason), Newhouser was even better. He lowered his ERA from 2.22 to 1.81, raised his strikeout total to 212 (no other pitcher in the major leagues had even 150), and allowed opponents just a .211 batting average and .535 OPS.

The Tigers won the pennant, and eventually the second World Series crown in franchise history, but Newhouser again had to win a close race against a teammate (second baseman Eddie Mayo this time) to take his second straight MVP.

Newhouser led the league in wins (25), ERA, and strikeouts, a pitching version of the Triple Crown that no Tiger would duplicate until Justin Verlander did it in his own MVP season of 2011.

Newhouser also won two games in the World Series, throwing a complete game in the Game 7 clincher at Wrigley Field, as the Tigers beat the Chicago Cubs.

That winter, a man named Jorge Pasquel offered Newhouser a $200,000 contract, and a $300,000 signing bonus, to jump to his Mexican League. It was huge money at the time, but it came with the risk of being banned from the major leagues, so Newhouser signed a $60,000 contract with the Tigers instead.

And if it hadn't been for Ted Williams, he would have won a third straight MVP. Williams came back from the war and hit .342 with 38 home runs, and his Boston Red Sox went 104–50. Newhouser went 26–9 with a 1.94 ERA, basically matching the totals he put up in the war years. He actually gave up fewer baserunners per inning than he had in either of the two MVP seasons, and his strikeout total (275 in 292²/₃ innings) was the highest of his career.

... allowed opponents a .211 average and .535 OPS.

Newhouser pitched for the Tigers for another six-plus seasons, but he developed arm problems in 1948 and was never really the same after that. The Tigers released him in the middle of the 1953 season, and while he came back the next year to pitch for the Cleveland Indians (where Greenberg was now the general manager), Newhouser was never a star again.

He made news later in life, when he was working as a scout for the Houston Astros and was pushing the Astros to draft a young shortstop from Kalamazoo named Derek Jeter. The Astros passed, and as the story goes, Newhouser resigned in protest. Other scouts in Michigan have suggested that Newhouser had planned to retire anyway (he was 71 years old), but it makes for a good story.

Newhouser's whole life makes for a good story, the story of the only pitcher who has ever won two straight MVPs.

And almost three.

Sparky Anderson's

5

Year Guarantee

Maybe it was a guarantee, maybe it wasn't. But there's no question that Sparky Anderson did say it, and there's no question he delivered on it.

In an interview on his first day as the Tigers' manager, Sparky said he'd have the team in the World Series before his five-year contract ran out. In 1984—exactly five years later—Sparky's Tigers won the fourth World Series title in franchise history.

By 1984, when the Tigers were a 104-win powerhouse and Alan Trammell and Lou Whitaker and Kirk Gibson and Jack Morris were all among the game's biggest stars, perhaps Sparky's prediction/guarantee didn't seem that bold. Then again, when Anderson took over the Tigers in June of 1979, they were a .500 team with nothing left from the championship team of 1968 and very little of what would become the title team of 1984.

Sparky's first Tiger roster did include Trammell, then a light-hitting 21-year-old shortstop who batted eighth. It included Lance Parrish, a 23-year-old catcher already beginning to show promise but not yet an All-Star. It included Dave Rozema, a 22-year-old starting pitcher who won 15 games as a rookie but had settled into what would be a so-so career.

As for the rest of the guys who played in that 3–2 loss to the Mariners, Sparky's first game with the Tigers, well, none of them would last with the Tigers until 1984. Several of them were out of baseball by then.

These weren't the 1970 Reds, the team of stars that Sparky rode to a World Series in his first season as a manager. The Tigers were a team that had some promising young talent, with more on the way, but they were also a team that would need plenty of hard work to have a chance at a championship.

"If Sparky would have known what he knew after he had taken the job, he probably wouldn't have taken it," Trammell would say years later. "He probably thought we were a little better prepared and had a little more talent than we actually did."

Perhaps, but the five-year "guarantee" was also all Sparky. He never minded a bold prediction.

Besides, as he told friends, "If we didn't win within five years, I knew I'd be out the door, anyway."

Instead, he ended up staying 17 years. He ended up winning 1,331 games in Detroit, easily the most of any manager in franchise history.

For a generation of fans, they weren't just the Tigers. They were "Sparky's Tigers."

And to think he almost ended up with the Cubs instead.

Anderson himself told the story in his 1998 book, *They Call Me Sparky,* co-authored with Dan Ewald, his longtime friend and PR man. He said he wasn't even planning on managing in 1979, after being fired by the Reds at the end of the 1978 season, but he was already choosing between six offers to take over a team in 1980.

MOST WINS AS TIGER MANAGER

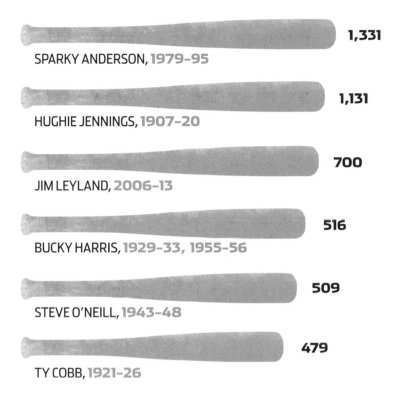

1,331
SPARKY ANDERSON, 1979–95

1,131
HUGHIE JENNINGS, 1907–20

700
JIM LEYLAND, 2006–13

516
BUCKY HARRIS, 1929–33, 1955–56

509
STEVE O'NEILL, 1943–48

479
TY COBB, 1921–26

None of those six offers was from the Tigers.

As Sparky tells it, he had pretty much settled on going to the Cubs, and was even negotiating his contract, when an off-hand comment to Don Drysdale made its way through George Kell and on to Tigers general manager Jim Campbell, who called and eventually talked Sparky into taking over—that very week.

"You only get a chance to hire a Sparky Anderson once," Campbell would say.

Sparky knew of the Tigers' young talent, in part because the Reds held their spring training in Tampa, Florida, and often played the

Tigers, who train in nearby Lakeland. Under the direction of Bill Lajoie, the Tigers had drafted Parrish in 1974, Whitaker in 1975, Trammell, Morris, and Dan Petry in 1976, and Gibson in 1978.

Later, they would add Darrell Evans as a free agent and Chet Lemon and Willie Hernandez in key trades. They improved to 92 wins by 1983, and began 1984 as a team that expected to win.

They would put together a team that remained a contender for the better part of a decade, and dominated all of baseball for one fantastic season. The '84 Tigers famously began the season by going 35–5, led the American League East wire to wire, and raced past the Royals and then the Padres to become champions.

... won 1,331 games in Detroit ... most in franchise history.

They made Sparky's prediction/guarantee come true. But even now, they'll all tell you that their manager might well have been the most important single piece of the puzzle.

"He was exactly what we needed," Trammell would say.

The Tigers were exactly what he needed, too. Sparky and Campbell began a relationship that only got closer, and lasted until the end of their lives. Sparky started a charity to support pediatric patients at Children's Hospital and Henry Ford Hospital in Detroit, and CATCH lives on and does great work even now that Anderson himself is gone.

Anderson didn't predict all that when he arrived in Detroit to take over a team that didn't look much like a champion.

He did say the Tigers would be back in the World Series, and he did say it would happen within the next five years.

And he did see that prediction come true.

Mickey Cochrane's

.582

Winning Percentage as Manager

It's hard to believe that Babe Ruth nearly became the Tigers manager. And harder to imagine what Tiger history would have looked like had it been Ruth, rather than Mickey Cochrane, who took over the Tigers in 1934.

It's hard to believe it would have been the same if owner Frank Navin got his first choice.

Navin wanted Ruth, because Ruth was the biggest name in the game. The Depression hit Detroit even worse than it hit other cities, and attendance was falling. The Tigers drew 869,318 in 1929, second in the American League. By 1933, they would draw just 320,972, fifth in what was then an eight-team league.

But as the story goes, Ruth made a trip to Hawaii, and Navin decided he couldn't wait for an answer. Connie Mack's Philadelphia

Athletics were also hurt by the Depression (and by a bank loan that was coming due), and Mack responded by selling off players from what only a few seasons before had been a championship team.

For $100,000, Navin could have Cochrane. He could have a new manager and a star catcher, all at the same time, even though at that point Cochrane still hadn't managed a game in his life.

Navin didn't have enough money, but his partner Walter O. Briggs did. Briggs helped finance the deal, and one of the best eras of Tigers baseball was born.

Cochrane took a team that hadn't won a pennant in 25 years, a team that hadn't even been in a pennant race in a decade and hadn't had an 80-win season in seven years, and transformed it.

He changed everything, turning the Tigers from losers into 101-game winners. And only one year later, in 1935, he gave the franchise its first-ever World Series title.

Meanwhile, he played so well that Cochrane himself was named the 1934 American League MVP. Had there been a Manager of the Year Award back then, Cochrane would have won that, too.

He only played for the Tigers for a little more than three seasons. He only managed the Tigers for another season or so after that.

Nine men have managed more games with the Tigers than Cochrane did. Nine men have more Tiger wins.

But no Tiger manager has ever had a better winning percentage than Black Mike's .582.

You could even argue that no Tiger manager has ever had a greater impact on the city and the franchise.

When Cochrane died in 1962, the *Detroit Free Press* wrote a glowing editorial.

"It has been said that Cochrane licked the depression in Detroit," the newspaper's editorial board wrote. "That's overstating it, naturally. But the man had a magic about him that made it easier for Detroit to ride out those early '30s. With the Tigers under

Cochrane, Detroit talked, thought, and lived baseball, and in so doing was at least partly able to forget its travail."

Not bad for a guy who liked football more than baseball at Boston University, back when he was known as Kid Cochrane. Not bad for a guy who at the start really didn't like catching at all.

"I didn't want to be a catcher," Cochrane told the *New York Times* in 1931, when he had already won his first MVP Award. "It was thrust upon me, as they say in the classics. I was in a fever to get out from behind the plate. Oh boy, I was terrible back there."

In his book, *Baseball: The Fans' Game,* Cochrane writes of wanting to move to the outfield. He also says that he first got the name Mickey when he played in the Pacific Coast League and his manager thought his given name of Gordon just wouldn't do.

"You're a Boston Irishman named Mickey Cochrane," Tom Turner told him, even though he wasn't exactly from Boston (he was from Bridgewater, Massachusetts) and he wasn't exactly Irish (his parents were of Scottish descent).

BEST WINNING PERCENTAGE, TIGER MANAGER
(MIN. 100 GAMES)

.582 Mickey Cochrane, 1934–38

.560 Mayo Smith, 1967–70

.556 Brad Ausmus, 2014

.551 Steve O'Neill, 1943–48

.549 Billy Martin, 1971–73

The "Black Mike" nickname would come later, a tribute to his gritty image but also a hint of the problems that would eventually help shorten Cochrane's Tiger career. While Cochrane was a great player and also a very successful manager, it was said that he had trouble with the spotlight and the pressure that came with it.

Just a year after the Tigers won the World Series, Cochrane had a nervous breakdown and had to take a break. He left the team to go to a ranch in Wyoming to recuperate.

Cochrane had problems of a different kind the next year, when he was hit on the head by a pitch from Bump Hadley of the New York Yankees. He nearly died, and never played another game.

He returned to manage the Tigers in 1938, but didn't make it through the season. He was fired on August 6, and never managed another major league game.

"We would have won more than just the one World Series if Mr. Briggs had left Cochrane alone to run the team," pitcher Elden Auker would write years later. "But he always wanted to put his stamp on it. He was a big fan and he thought he knew how to run the team better than Cochrane did."

We'll never know what could have been if Briggs had done as Auker (and presumably others) hoped. We'll never know what Cochrane might have done had he stayed healthy, mentally and physically.

And we'll never know if the Tigers could have done as well under Babe Ruth as they did under Mickey Cochrane.

We do know that in the 115 seasons the Tigers have been playing baseball, no manager has ever won games at a better rate than Cochrane.

And perhaps no manager ever meant more to a city.

Bill Lajoie Drafts

5

All-Stars in 1976

The 1968 Tigers were from a different era. Not only were they the last team to win a World Series without first going through a League Championship Series—the last real world champions, some would say—but they were also one of the last title teams built almost entirely with players signed as amateur free agents.

Baseball only went to a draft system in 1965, and only two '68 Tigers (relievers Jon Warden and Les Cain) were signed as draft picks. Not only was the draft a fairly recent development, but the Tigers hadn't come close to figuring out the new system of acquiring talent.

In fact, for the first nine years the draft was held (1965–73), the Tigers didn't draft and sign a single player who would become a major league All-Star. Their drafts produced few big-league players of any kind.

That all changed in 1974, and it changed because general manager Jim Campbell was smart enough to turn over his scouting system over to a 39-year-old Detroit native named Bill Lajoie.

Lajoie was a high school star at Denby, and a college star at Western Michigan, but his 10-year professional career stalled in Triple-A. He would go on to make a much bigger impact as an executive, beginning with the job he did building the team that would win the 1984 World Series.

And it all began when Campbell offered Lajoie a $15,000 salary to take over for Ed Katalinas as the Tigers' scouting director.

> **Jack Morris was only 4-6 with a 4.72 ERA in his junior season at Brigham Young.**

Lajoie's first draft brought in Lance Parrish and Mark Fidrych. The next year he picked Dave Rozema, Tom Brookens, Jason Thompson, and Lou Whitaker.

Not bad, but the best was still to come. In 1976, Lajoie's Tigers would bring in the best draft haul in franchise history, and one of the best in the history of any franchise. Twenty-four years later, Baseball America would rank the Tigers' 1976 draft as the second-best in history. The only one rated better was the 1968 Los Angeles Dodgers draft that included Steve Garvey, Ron Cey, Bill Buckner, and Bobby Valentine.

So who did the Tigers draft in 1976?

Only two of the best shortstops of our era, a starting pitcher who should be in the Hall of Fame and another who would pitch in the majors for 13 seasons, an All-Star outfielder the Tigers would eventually trade for another All-Star, and eight other players who would log big-league time.

That's all. Just Alan Trammell, Ozzie Smith, Jack Morris, Dan Petry, Steve Kemp, Pat Underwood, Roger Weaver, Kip Young, Dave Stegman, and Glenn Gulliver.

Smith, of course, did not sign with the Tigers. In his book, *Character Is Not a Statistic,* Lajoie wrote that he only lost Ozzie because Campbell wouldn't allow him to raise the Tigers' offer from $10,000 to $15,000.

Imagine Ozzie Smith AND Alan Trammell with the Tigers. Imagine an infield with Trammell, Whitaker...and Ozzie.

Alas, that didn't happen. But even without Ozzie, Lajoie's '76 draft class would be the most significant the Tigers have ever had. In an era when the Tigers still didn't believe much in free agency, Lajoie's astute drafting was the only reason the Tigers even had a chance to build a team that would win a World Series.

Trammell, Morris, Petry, and Kemp would all make the All-Star team as Tigers, and all but Kemp would play huge roles on the '84 champions. Kemp did, too, in his own way, because Lajoie (by then the Tigers general manager) would trade him to the Chicago White Sox for Chet Lemon after the 1981 season.

What makes Lajoie's '76 draft even more impressive is that none of his five All-Stars was an obvious, automatic pick. In fact, the most heralded player the Tigers picked that year was Underwood, a high school left-hander out of Indiana who they chose second overall (first overall pick Floyd Bannister went to the Houston Astros). Underwood appeared in 113 games for the Tigers. He was traded to the Cincinnati Reds midway through the 1983 season for Wayne Krenchicki (who was sold back to the Reds after the season).

> *... none of Lajoie's five All-Stars was an obvious, automatic pick.*

Kemp, chosen with the first overall pick in the January draft (teams drafted twice a season until 1987), was also considered a big-time prospect, said by his college coach at USC to be a better player than reigning American League MVP Fred Lynn.

But Trammell wasn't even the highest-profile high school infielder in Southern California (an honor that scouts gave to Glenn

Hoffman). Jack Morris was only 4–6 with a 4.72 ERA in his junior season at Brigham Young. Petry was a 6' high school right-hander who had yet to mature into the pitcher he would become.

Oh, and Ozzie Smith was a 5'10", 135-pound second baseman at Cal Poly San Luis Obispo.

Lajoie relied on scout Dick Wiencek, who recommended and signed Trammell, Petry, and Morris. Wiencek thought Trammell would hit .260 and play strong defense at shortstop (even Wiencek underestimated Trammell). Wiencek noticed Morris when he went to see Bannister pitch, and Morris' BYU team just happened to be the opponent.

Morris lost but pitched well that day. His overall college numbers weren't great, but Lajoie loved that he was at his best in the biggest games, against the best opposition.

Somehow, Lajoie and his scouts were able to spot things that others didn't, to identify players that other teams were passing over.

The Tigers would draft Kirk Gibson in 1978, the same year Lajoie also picked Marty Castillo in the fifth round. Gibson and Castillo would be among the nine 1984 Tigers who arrived via Lajoie draft picks. Seven more would be added in trades for players Lajoie chose in the draft.

There was more work to do to build a champion. Lajoie would trade for Lemon, Larry Herndon, Dave Bergman, Aurelio Lopez, and Willie Hernandez, and would buy Milt Wilcox from the Chicago Cubs. The Tigers would sign Darrell Evans and Juan Berenguer as free agents.

They would hire Sparky Anderson as manager, and watch Anderson put it all together.

None of it would have happened without those early Lajoie drafts. None of it would have happened without that 1976 draft, the best draft the Tigers ever had and one of the best drafts any team ever had.

Jack Morris'

11

Consecutive Opening Day Starts

As Roger Craig liked to put it, there are Opening Day pitchers, and pitchers who start on Opening Day.

"Jack Morris is probably the best of the former," Craig wrote in *Inside Pitch,* his 1984 book with Vern Plagenhoef. "Better than Don Drysdale, Jim Bunning, Bob Gibson, Sandy Koufax, Don Newcombe, and Carl Erskine."

You can argue where Morris should rank on a list of baseball's best pitchers—his many near-misses in Hall of Fame voting stand as evidence that plenty do argue—but Morris' status among those who played with him remains unchallenged. In a big game, they all wanted Jack Morris on the mound.

Year after year, when Jack Morris was on the staff, there were never any questions about who was the ace.

He was the guy you wanted on the mound in Game 1 in October. He was definitely the guy you wanted on the mound in Game 7 in October.

And he was always on the mound on Opening Day, for 11 consecutive years with the Tigers (beginning in 1980, when he threw a complete game three-hitter to beat the Royals), and then for three more years with the Minnesota Twins and Toronto Blue Jays.

Only Tom Seaver started more Opening Day games than Morris. The only pitcher in history with more Opening Day wins than Morris' eight was Walter Johnson, who had nine of his 417 career wins on Opening Day, and was one of the charter members of the Hall of Fame.

Morris' no-hitter was the first by a Tiger in 26 years.

Had Morris been as good in every game as he was on Opening Day (his 11-start ERA of 2.85 was a run better than his overall ERA), he would have sailed into the Hall of Fame.

Not bad for a guy who became a Tiger because scout Dick Wiencek wanted to see Floyd Bannister pitch.

Longtime Tiger executive Bill Lajoie tells the story in his book, *Character Is Not a Statistic.* Wiencek and many other scouts had gone to a tournament in Riverside, California, to watch Bannister, the Arizona State left-hander who would end up as the top overall pick (by the Houston Astros) in that 1976 draft.

As Lajoie wrote, "Wiencek would indeed find the Tigers' future ace that day. It just wasn't Bannister."

Morris was pitching for Brigham Young, and he lost that matchup with Bannister, 4–0. But as Wiencek later told Lajoie, "Morris battled Bannister pitch for pitch, and wasn't the least bit intimidated by going against the best pitcher and the best team in college baseball."

MOST OPENING DAY WINS

Walter Johnson

Jack Morris

Grover Cleveland Alexander

Tom Seaver

Randy Johnson

Jimmy Key

Anyone who has met Jack Morris, or maybe even anyone who watched him pitch in a big-league career that would span 18 seasons, can fully understand that Morris was never going to be intimidated by anyone.

Lajoie mentions phoning Gordon Lakey, who at that time was working for the Major League Scouting Bureau. Lakey had also scouted that start against Bannister and ASU.

"I'm sold on [Morris]," Lakey told Lajoie.

Eight years later, Lakey was working in the major leagues, and was on hand at Minnesota's Metrodome when Morris opened the 1984 season with an 8–1 win over the Twins. Lakey saw Craig after the game, and told the Tiger pitching coach that Morris had "no-hit stuff."

You might remember what happened four days later in Chicago.

It wasn't Opening Day, but it was a big stage, with Morris facing a team that won 99 games and the American League West title the year before. It was the nationally-televised Saturday Game of the Week, back when that distinction still meant something.

It was also, amazingly enough, Jack Morris against Floyd Bannister, the same pitching matchup that helped make Morris a Tiger.

The score, once again, was 4–0, but this time there wasn't any question about which pitcher was No. 1. Morris threw a no-hitter, the first by a Tiger in 26 years and the only one by a Tiger pitcher between Jim Bunning in 1958 and Justin Verlander in 2007.

Radar guns were just coming into use then, so there are no records of Morris' pitch speeds that day. But Craig said that with the focus of national TV and the lure of a big game, Morris seemed to throw harder than usual that day against the White Sox.

He never threw a no-hitter on Opening Day. The closest he came was that three-hitter in his first Opening Day start in 1980 in Kansas City.

More often than not, though, Morris pitched very well in the first game of the year. More often than not, he won.

He's probably best remembered for the night he pitched the final game of the baseball season, the 10-inning, 1–0 shutout for the Twins over the Atlanta Braves in Game 7 of the 1991 World Series.

It was the closing game, not the opening one. But it was the type of game that called for an Opening Day pitcher.

Few were ever better in that role than Jack Morris.

Kirk Gibson's

4

20–20 Seasons

Kirk Gibson wasn't a .300 hitter. He never drove in 100 runs in a season, and he never played in an All-Star Game (although at least in one instance, that was his choice).

The usual ways of evaluating baseball players left Gibson looking very average. Even modern metrics didn't help, with Gibson only once finishing in the top 10 in his league in baseball-reference. com's version of wins above replacement (WAR).

Kirk Gibson wasn't average, and anyone who watched him play knew it. He would beat you, and he would do it in many ways, and perhaps the one real way to demonstrate that is with his 20–20 seasons.

Twenty home runs. Twenty stolen bases.

Plenty of players get one or the other. In the history of the Tigers before 1984, no one had done both in the same year.

Then Kirk Gibson did it—four years in a row.

He actually did it five years in a row, but the fifth was in 1988, and it wasn't with the Tigers. Owner Tom Monaghan and club president Jim Campbell didn't want to pay Gibson what the outfielder thought he was worth, and after first demanding that general manager Bill Lajoie trade Gibson, Campbell watched Gibson run away to the Los Angeles Dodgers as a free agent.

An arbitrator had ruled Gibson free, as a result of the players' collusion case against the owners. Gibson signed with the Dodgers for $4.5 million over three years, although he later said he had told the Tigers he would have taken $500,000 less to stay.

Gibson went west and became an MVP and World Series hero. The Tigers went into a nosedive they wouldn't recover from for nearly two decades.

MOST 20–20 SEASONS BY A TIGER

Kirk Gibson

Alan Trammell

Curtis Granderson

Gary Sheffield

Chad Curtis

Damion Easley

It wasn't all because they let Kirk Gibson leave. But anyone who watched him play realized that losing him sure didn't help.

Gibson was an amazing athlete, a "breathtaking prospect" out of Michigan State, in the words of Kansas City Royals scouting legend Art Stewart.

"I'm telling you, this guy could do it all," Stewart wrote in his book, *The Art of Scouting.* "He was a guy who really made your heart beat."

... Gibson signed with the Dodgers for $4.5 million over three years.

He could run faster than anyone else. He could hit the ball farther than anyone else.

The Major League Scouting Bureau report on him in 1978 listed him with 80 speed and 80 power. In scouting terms, 80 means Hall of Fame level. As Lajoie wrote in his own book, *Character is Not a Statistic,* it means "Ron LeFlore's speed with Willie Stargell's power."

He really did look like "the next Mickey Mantle," even if Sparky Anderson would later admit that the comparison was a little unfair.

As it turned out, Gibson never stole 97 bases in a season, as LeFlore did. He never hit 48 home runs in a season, as Stargell did. Baseball is still looking for the next Mickey Mantle.

But the next Kirk Gibson wouldn't be bad, either.

"Gibby will probably never go into the Hall of Fame, but he was a Hall of Fame performer," Anderson wrote in his book, *They Call Me Sparky.* "Gibby was a true winner. He's the perfect team player."

Gibson could beat you with his legs, he could beat you with his determination and he sure as heck could beat you with his power, as Goose Gossage and Dennis Eckersley were reminded when Gibson hit two of the more memorable home runs in World Series history.

Kirk Gibson celebrates after hitting his second home run of Game 5 of the 1984 World Series. *(Sporting News/Getty Images)*

It took a while for it all to develop. Gibson was in the big leagues by age 22, but he wasn't a big-league regular until he was 26. He wasn't a big star until he was 27, helping lead the '84 Tigers with the first of those 20–20 seasons.

It was still something of a big deal then, a combination of power and speed that only the best athletes could match. Hank Aaron and Willie Mays could. Mantle, too, although his knee problems slowed him enough that he only reached 20–20 once.

No one had ever done it with the Tigers. Only six Tigers had even gone 15–15.

And while five other Tigers have gone 20–20 since Gibson did it the first time, it's still true today that no Tiger has done it nearly as often as Gibson did.

He'll be remembered by Tiger fans more for the home run against Gossage, or for any number of other big home runs. He'll be remembered for the way he played the game, for the home-plate collisions.

He'll be remembered for the photo with his arms in the air in celebration.

But if you're looking for a statistic to remember Kirk Gibson by, 20–20 isn't bad.

Alan Trammell's

9

Hits in the 1984 World Series

Far too often, Alan Trammell got overlooked.

He should have been the American League's MVP in 1987, but he narrowly lost out to George Bell. He should be in the Hall of Fame, but voters keep passing him by.

Sure, Trammell got noticed. He played 20 years in the big leagues. He managed the Tigers for three years. It's not that he was anonymous.

But he should have gotten more credit than he did.

Even for what he did in the 1984 World Series.

Trammell was named the MVP that October, as he should have been. He was 9 for 20 in the five World Series games. In Game 4, when a Padres win would have evened the Series, it was Trammell whose two home runs accounted for all the runs in a 4–2 Tigers win.

Does anyone even remember?

There's only one home run from that October they ever show, only one home run anyone ever talks about. It's a great video, that one of Sparky Anderson laughing in the dugout and Kirk Gibson teeing off on Goose Gossage. It's a great image, of Gibson with his arms in the air.

And it was no more important than the two home runs Alan Trammell hit the day before. Less important, really, when you think about it.

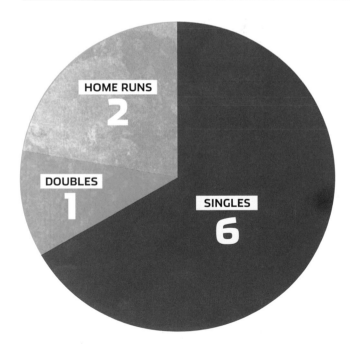

ALAN TRAMMELL'S 9 HITS IN THE 1984 WORLD SERIES

HOME RUNS
2

DOUBLES
1

SINGLES
6

Alan Trammell hits a home run during Game 4 of the 1984 World Series.
(Ronald C. Modra)

Not that you'd ever get Trammell to say it bothered him. Remember, this is a guy who signed an undervalued seven-year contract for $2.6 million, and never complained about it.

"I have two houses, I take care of my wife and son, I'm putting money away," Trammell said during the '84 Series. "I should be set for life. What more do you want?"

He was a proud baseball lifer, then and now. He was a great player who never wanted to take off the uniform, happy to teach the game as a coach when he got too old to play.

Trammell sneaked into Padres games as a kid growing up in San Diego, then played against the Padres in his only World Series. The Tigers were favorites, the team that began the season 35–5 and led the American League East from wire to wire, the team that swept past the Royals in the AL playoffs.

As MVP, Trammell was 9 for 20 in the five World Series games.

The Padres were the team that shouldn't have been there, the team that kept America from a dream Tigers-Cubs matchup by rallying from a two-games-to-none deficit in the best-of-five NL playoffs.

"We want the Cubs! We want the Cubs!" the Tiger Stadium fans had chanted, as the Tigers wrapped up their playoff sweep of the Royals.

It wasn't the Cubs. It was the Padres, and it ended up being a World Series that much of America has forgotten, even if it's one that will live on forever for Tiger fans.

Trammell put the Tigers ahead right from the start, following Lou Whitaker's leadoff double in Game 1 with a base hit that gave the Tigers their first run. He had two hits in that game, and two more the next day, in the only game the Tigers lost.

He was on base four times in Game 3, a 5–2 Tiger win, with a second-inning double that drove in a run. And then he dominated Game 4 with three more hits, including the two-run home runs, in the first inning and the third. He was just the second shortstop ever with two homers in a World Series game (Rico Petrocelli did it for the 1967 Red Sox), a distinction he still holds 30 years later.

"When I got to second base [in the fifth inning], Tim Flannery called me Babe Ruth," Trammell told reporters that day. "Then Garry Templeton said he wanted to brush against me, it might rub off, he might get hot."

Even with that, there were many who thought Jack Morris (two complete-game wins, four runs allowed in 18 innings) should have been named MVP. Even with that, it's the Gibson home run that keeps getting replayed, year after year.

But it really was Tram's Series, the one he played with a bad shoulder and a bad knee that would require surgery, the one he played in the ballpark he grew up with.

"I had never played at Jack Murphy Stadium before," he told author George Cantor years later. "To be on that field for my first World Series... isn't that what you dream of when you're a kid who loves baseball?"

It was his first World Series. It was his only World Series.

But at least it was his World Series—Tram's World Series.

Mickey Lolich's

3

World Series Wins in 1968

He didn't win 31 games, and he didn't have a 1.12 ERA. He's not Denny McLain and he's not Bob Gibson, and maybe that's why we haven't spent the past half-century talking about what Mickey Lolich did in 1968.

All he did was win three games in the World Series. All he did was come back on just two days' rest to beat Gibson, in St. Louis, in Game 7.

It didn't seem nearly as unusual at the time as a pitcher winning 31 games (as McLain did) or completing a season with a 1.12 ERA (as Gibson did). Gibson had won three World Series games just the year before, Sandy Koufax had won Game 7 on two days' rest in 1965, and Gibson did it the year before that.

But just as no one has won 31 games in a season since 1968, and just as no one has had a 1.12 ERA since 1968, no one has started and won three games in a single World Series since then, either.

No one has started and won Game 7 on two days' rest since then, and certainly no one has won three games in a World Series, and started and won Game 7 on two days' rest while beating a pitcher who had a 1.12 ERA that season.

"All my life, somebody has been a big star and Lolich was No. 2," Mickey told reporters that day. "I figured my day would come, and this was it."

He was named the World Series MVP, but a funny thing has happened in the decades since. The 1968 World Series has come to be remembered for everything and everyone but Mickey Lolich.

... only the third time since *1920* *a pitcher had* **three** **complete-game** *wins in the World Series.*

Gibson's 17-strikeout masterpiece in Game 1 gets more attention. Willie Horton throwing out Lou Brock at the plate in Game 5 gets more attention. Mayo Smith's decision to play Mickey Stanley at shortstop gets more attention. So does Jose Feliciano's singing of the national anthem, and Al Kaline's .379 average.

Even Jim Northrup's two-run triple to break a scoreless tie in the seventh inning of Game 7 gets more attention.

Not that it shouldn't.

It's just that as the years go on, what Lolich did that October looks more and more impressive. It's like his innings totals, the 376 he threw in 1971 or the 330 he averaged in four seasons from 1971–74, which look more stunning now than they did then.

The Tigers of Lolich's era said they always had to convince Mickey how good he could be. It's as if now we all need to look back to remind ourselves how good he was.

And how great, and unexpected, his World Series performance in 1968 was.

MOST WORLD SERIES WINS, TIGERS

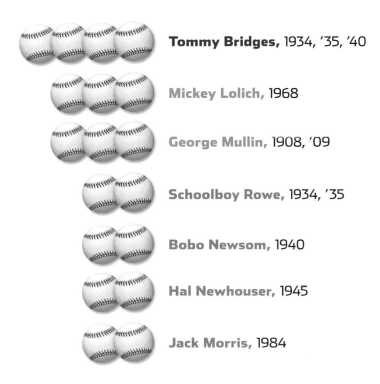

Tommy Bridges, 1934, '35, '40

Mickey Lolich, 1968

George Mullin, 1908, '09

Schoolboy Rowe, 1934, '35

Bobo Newsom, 1940

Hal Newhouser, 1945

Jack Morris, 1984

Lolich was a good pitcher in 1968, but he hardly looked unbeatable. He was pulled from the rotation for the first three weeks of August, after a five-start stretch where he had a 7.25 ERA (even worse than it sounds, given what a low-scoring game baseball was in '68).

His Game 2 win over the Cardinals was described by the *New York Times* as a "stunningly rounded effort," and not just because that day Lolich hit the only home run he would ever hit in the big leagues. His nine strikeouts didn't come close to matching the 17 Gibson had the day before, but Lolich allowed just six hits in an 8–1 complete-game win.

McLain lost to Gibson in Game 1, and again in Game 4, so when Lolich took the mound for Game 5 at Tiger Stadium, he was pitching to save his team's season. He did—with another complete-game win—but he did more than that. In a game that would be remembered for Horton's throw and for Kaline's two-run single that gave the Tigers the lead in the seventh, it was Lolich's one-out single that began that winning rally.

With the Tigers down 3–2 and just eight outs to go, Lolich probably shouldn't have even been allowed to bat in the seventh. But Smith was an unconventional manager, and in 1968 whatever he did was going to work.

MICKEY LOLICH'S HIGHEST INNINGS TOTALS

1971 ▶ **376**

1972 ▶ **327¹/₃**

1973 ▶ **308²/₃**

1974 ▶ **308**

The Game 5 win gave Smith another big decision to make. His first thought was to start Earl Wilson or Joe Sparma in Game 6, but McLain said after Game 5 that he wanted to pitch it. Smith agreed, and McLain won, although with the Tigers scoring 13 runs (10 of them in the third inning), it may not have mattered who pitched.

Sometime during that game, Smith approached Lolich about starting Game 7. Mickey wasn't sure about pitching on two days' rest, but Smith asked him, "Do you think you can pitch five [innings]?"

The Cardinals believed Lolich would tire. They knew Gibson would beat him.

Gibson thought so, too.

"I was absolutely sure we were going to win that game," he said. "I knew Lolich wasn't exactly what you'd call a finely tuned athlete. He had to be dog-tired coming back on two days' rest. I was tired, too, but I'd been through this before."

The Tigers weren't nearly as surprised. They knew that Lolich was different from other pitchers, that he could throw every day.

"He was a freak," said Jim Price, the backup catcher on that 1968 team. "He could throw 12 pitches and be ready to pitch in the game. He never ran. He always said, 'I don't run the ball to the plate.'"

He threw it, and he threw it hard. There were no radar guns in those days, but Price figures Lolich's fastball would have been clocked in the mid-90s.

Gibson's *17-strikeout masterpiece in Game 1 gets more attention ...*

Anyway, in Game 7, tired or not, Lolich was brilliant. He helped himself with two pickoffs, but he allowed only five hits in a 4–1 complete-game win. It was only the third time since 1920 that a pitcher had three complete-game wins in the same World Series (Lew Burdette in 1957, Gibson in 1967), and needless to say, it hasn't been matched since.

For being named the World Series MVP, Lolich was presented with a Dodge Charger, but he told reporters that his wife would be taking the car. Lolich preferred motorcycles, anyway, but once again it seemed he was No. 2—even when he was the MVP.

Dave Dombrowski's

21

July Trades

Not every trade Dave Dombrowski has made for the Tigers was a great one. Not every one was even good.

All that does is make Dombrowski's record more impressive. All that does is prove what we already know, which is that the Tigers general manager never operates in fear that a deal won't work out.

And really, that's one of the biggest reasons that so many of them do.

Dombrowski is never fearful of being bold. He's never fearful of trading touted prospects. He never works in fear of anything, which is why he ends up making the big moves that so many other GMs would pull back from.

You'll never hear Dombrowski justify inaction by a general claim that "prices are too high." You'll never hear him say he didn't get anything done because other teams just weren't aggressive enough.

He's always aggressive. He's always relentless. And more often than not, he's the one who ends up making the exact trade that the Tigers needed.

Two of his best Tiger trades came not in July, but in December, at baseball's winter meetings. He went to Nashville in 2007 and came back with Miguel Cabrera, even though the cost was Cameron Maybin and Andrew Miller, who at the time were his two most-prized prospects. He went to Indianapolis in 2009 and came back with Max Scherzer, even though the questions at the time were about how he could trade away Curtis Granderson.

Dombrowski has made 21 July trades in 13 seasons as GM.

The December meetings are a key time for any general manager, but July might be even bigger. December is about building a team. July is about taking a team that could win and finding the piece or pieces to put it over the top.

July is when Dombrowski has made 21 trades in 13 seasons as Tigers general manager.

July is about pestering the Seattle Mariners all month to get Doug Fister in 2011, because the market that year was thin in starting pitchers and the Tigers absolutely had to have one.

"Over a three-week period, we called a couple of times a day," Dombrowski said later that year. "Sometimes three times. [Mariners general manager Jack Zduriencik] opened the door at times, and then he would close it. As long as it was open a little, we kept trying."

Fister went 8–1 with a 1.79 ERA down the stretch, and added two more wins in that postseason. None of the players Dombrowski gave up in the deal have turned out to be great, but he would tell you that isn't the proper way to judge a trade.

"I never understood the idea that you could get talent without giving up talent," Dombrowski likes to say.

He won't trade just anyone. He never dealt Justin Verlander. But if Dombrowski likes what he's getting back, you'll never hear him complain too loudly over what he had to give up.

His first July trade with the Tigers was a complicated three-way deal with the New York Yankees and Oakland A's. The 2002 Tigers were far from being contenders, and Dombrowski was trying to acquire young talent while shipping out older players he didn't want. Jeff Weaver went to the Yankees and Carlos Pena came from the A's, but the key to the deal was a player to be named later who turned out to be Jeremy Bonderman.

The first year the Tigers had a chance to win under Dombrowski was 2006. They needed a hitter at midseason, and at the deadline he got Sean Casey from the Pittsburgh Pirates.

Casey didn't do all that well, at least not until the World Series, when he hit .529 against the St. Louis Cardinals. If his teammates had done a little better—or if the Tigers hadn't had a week off before the Series, or if the pitchers hadn't committed so many blasted errors—Casey might well have been the team's World Series hero.

Dombrowski got Kyle Farnsworth in 2008 (didn't work out), and Jarrod Washburn in 2009 (ditto). But he got Jhonny Peralta in 2010 (that worked), and Fister the year after that (yes, worked).

Then in 2012, the Tigers found themselves in need of a second baseman and another starting pitcher. Dombrowski found both in the same place, getting Anibal Sanchez and Omar Infante from the Miami Marlins.

Sanchez became a postseason star, with a 1.77 ERA in three October starts as the Tigers went to the World Series. A year later, he won the American League ERA title.

But at midseason 2013, the Tigers had another big need. They knew Peralta was facing a suspension for his part in the Biogenesis scandal, and they didn't have a satisfactory replacement available.

Dombrowski struck again, getting Jose Iglesias in a three-way deal with the Boston Red Sox and Chicago White Sox.

July 2014 provided a perfect example of how Dombrowski keeps working. He needed a reliever, and he got Joakim Soria from the Texas Rangers. But even though starting pitcher didn't seem to be the Tigers' biggest need, he knew what an impact David Price could make. So Dombrowski kept at it with the Tampa Bay Rays, and on deadline day he landed the 2012 AL Cy Young winner in yet another three-way trade.

Sanchez became a star, ... 1.77 ERA in three October starts

With Price, Verlander, and Scherzer, the Tigers had the last three AL Cy Young winners in the same rotation. Dombrowski had traded for two of them.

Not every deal Dombrowski pursues ends up getting done. Before trading for Iglesias, he pursued Jurickson Profar of the Rangers.

But he keeps trying. He always keeps trying, long after many other general managers have thrown up their hands and declared that they tried hard but couldn't get anything done.

Dombrowski keeps at it, knowing that there will be a cost involved, but also knowing there's rarely a reward without the willingness to pay that cost.

"We've got to win," he said after paying the price for Price. "That's what it comes down to. If we win, then I'll be very satisfied."

David Price Strikes Out

10

(and Walks None) in Tiger Debut

Dave Dombrowski wasn't looking to trade for a starting pitcher in July of 2014. A shaky bullpen was the big problem that needed fixing. Another bat wouldn't be bad.

A starter? The Tigers had five good starters.

Then they watched David Price pitch for the Tampa Bay Rays at Comerica Park 3½ weeks before the non-waiver trade deadline. And then a few people on Dombrowski's staff had the same thought.

Why not David Price?

The more they thought, the more sense it made. Why not see if they could trade for Price, the best player available on the July market? Why not add Price to a rotation that already included Max Scherzer, Justin Verlander, Anibal Sanchez and Rick Porcello? Why not have Price as protection in the likelihood that Scherzer would leave as a free agent after 2014 (as he did)?

Why not?

Even for Dombrowski, who specializes in the big trade and in the big July trade, this one was something special. He worked and worked, and after a three-team deal that also involved the Seattle Mariners, Price became a Tiger.

Five days later at Yankee Stadium, Price made Tiger history, becoming the first pitcher ever with 10 strikeouts and no walks in his Tiger debut. It was major league history, too, because Price was only the second pitcher since 1900 to switch teams and debut with double-digit strikeouts and no walks (John Henry Johnson with the 1979 Texas Rangers was the other).

*Price was the 2nd pitcher since **1900** to switch teams and debut with double-digit strikeouts and no walks.*

"Same pitcher, different uniform," Yankees left fielder Brett Gardner said. "I would prefer he went to the National League."

The Yankees were all too familiar with Price, who won the 2012 Cy Young while pitching in the American League East for the Rays. But now he was a Tiger, joining a unique rotation that also featured the 2011 (Verlander) and 2013 (Scherzer) Cy Young winners.

"He is like an old-fashioned power pitcher," Derek Jeter said that night. "He throws 98, and he doesn't walk you."

Price's double-digit strikeout, no-walk game against the Yankees was the ninth of his career. That's as many as Bob Gibson had, more than Nolan Ryan had.

It was just the 29th game like that in the entire history of the Tigers. No Tiger pitcher had more than five (Scherzer and Mickey Lolich).

Price did it in his first game.

"He was calm, he was methodical, he got outs," manager Brad Ausmus said.

He didn't win, leaving in the ninth inning with the score tied 3–3. But the Tigers won, scoring a run in the 12th to beat the Yankees, 4–3.

Price gave the Tigers something they have rarely had, a power-pitching left-hander. Lolich and Hal Newhouser are the only Tiger lefties with 10 or more double-digit strikeout games; Price had two in his first seven Tiger starts.

He had 23 of them in his 6½ seasons with the Rays. Among American League pitchers, only Felix Hernandez, Yu Darvish, and Verlander (all right-handers) had more in that span.

Price did everything the Rays expected, everything they could have asked, after Tampa Bay made him the first pick overall in the 2007 draft. He was in the big leagues a year later, a September call-up who became a key relief pitcher in the playoffs, helping the Rays to their only World Series.

By 2010, Price was a 24-year-old All-Star, a 19-game winner who finished second to Hernandez in AL Cy Young voting. By 2012, he won 20 games and also won the Cy Young, and the only problem

MOST DOUBLE-DIGIT STRIKEOUT GAMES, TIGERS

54	28	25	24	22
Mickey Lolich	Justin Verlander	Jack Morris	Jim Bunning	Max Scherzer

the small-budget Rays had was that they knew they could never afford to sign him long-term.

In 2010, Price finished **SECOND** in AL Cy Young voting.

There was never a question that the Rays would trade him. The only issue was when, and to which team. The Tigers paid attention, as just about every team in baseball did, but it was hard to find anyone who believed they were the team that would get him. That was as true as ever in July 2014, if only because no one was expecting the Tigers to trade for a starting pitcher.

They weren't going to trade for just any starter. They had five that they liked.

But David Price isn't just any starter, and the Tigers realized they could get him for a cost they could live with.

At that point, it was a simple question.

Why not?

Anibal Sanchez
Strikes Out

17

Anibal Sanchez thought he had escaped the Atlanta Braves.

They were the one team in the National League East that always gave him trouble when he pitched for the Marlins, the team he'd lost to 11 times in 17 starts, with a 5.42 ERA he would just as soon forget. The July 2012 trade that brought Sanchez to the Tigers was a blessing in many ways, for him and for the Tigers, but it certainly didn't bother Sanchez to be leaving the Braves behind as he switched to the American League.

Then the 2013 schedule came out, and sure enough, the Braves were one of the Tigers' interleague opponents. Sure enough, the rotation worked out so that Sanchez would pitch the series opener on a late April Friday night at Comerica Park.

It would turn into one of the most memorable nights of the Tigers' season, and certainly of Sanchez's major league career. But the day before the game, he wasn't so sure.

"I was talking to [Justin] Verlander about it," Sanchez remembered a year later. "I told him I'd had problems with Atlanta, that my ERA against them was high. He said, 'You're more mature. You're a different pitcher now.'

"The next day I struck out 17, and he said, 'See?'"

We all saw.

That night, April 27, 2013, Anibal Sanchez wrote his name into the Tigers record book. He became the first pitcher in Tiger history to strike out 17 batters in a game, breaking a 44-year-old record that Mickey Lolich set in May 1969 and equaled two weeks later.

Sanchez pitched eight shutout innings, in a 10–0 Tiger win. He allowed just five hits and had only one walk, but the story that night was the 17 strikeouts.

TOP STRIKEOUT GAMES IN TIGER HISTORY

17
ANIBAL SANCHEZ VS. BRAVES, 4/26/2013

16
MICKEY LOLICH VS. PILOTS, 6/9/1969

16
MICKEY LOLICH VS. ANGELS, 5/23/1969

15
MAX SCHERZER VS. PIRATES, 5/20/2012

15
MICKEY LOLICH VS. RED SOX, 10/2/1972

15
PAUL FOYTACK VS. SENATORS, 7/28/1956

The Tigers have had plenty of high-profile, high-strikeout pitchers. Verlander and Max Scherzer finished 1–2 in the major leagues in strikeouts in 2012, with Sanchez tied for 33rd. Scherzer would finish second again in 2013. Tiger pitchers have led the American League in strikeouts 12 times (13 if you include David Price's 2014 season, split between Tampa Bay and Detroit).

But on one April night, against the team that had given Anibal Sanchez more trouble than any other opponent, Sanchez would be the strikeout king.

Perhaps we shouldn't have been surprised.

The Braves were a different team in 2012, a team that would strike out nearly 1,400 times for the season. They had signed B.J. Upton and traded for his brother Justin, and both would fan more than 150 times. Dan Uggla had turned into a strikeout machine.

But Verlander was also right. Anibal Sanchez was a different pitcher that year, and especially that night.

"Everything worked," pitching coach Jeff Jones would remember.

Sanchez tends to throw his fastball at 90–92 mph, but that night he averaged 95 and had one pitch clocked at 96.9 mph, according to brooksbaseball.net. His changeup was outstanding, and the Braves were chasing both that pitch and his backdoor slider with regularity.

He struck out Uggla and Justin Upton in the first inning, and Freddie Freeman, Evan Gattis, and Juan Francisco in the second. He would get Uggla four times and Freeman three before the night was over.

Sanchez threw 30 changeups, and the Braves swung and missed at 12 of them, seven for strike three. He got 14 of the 17 strikeouts on a swinging third strike.

He threw 121 pitches, nearly 70 percent of them for strikes. And the Braves put just 11 of them in play.

"It was boring," right fielder Torii Hunter told reporters that night. "Standing out there was boring. But at the same time, it was awesome. The later he stayed out there, the more intense it got."

Sanchez equaled his own career high of 14 when he fanned Chris Johnson for the second out of the seventh inning. He tied Lolich's Tiger record by getting Juan Francisco and Reed Johnson to begin the eighth. He finished the night with an 81 mph curveball, one of the few he threw all game, to get Uggla a fourth time, and set a new Tiger record.

Anibal Sanchez walks off the field after striking out Dan Uggla for his 17th strikeout, which ended the eighth inning. *(Photo Courtesy AP Photo/Paul Sancya)*

While he wouldn't have another strikeout night like that one against the Braves, Sanchez would go on to have one of the most overlooked great seasons by a Tiger pitcher. A month later, he would take a no-hit bid into the ninth inning against the Twins, before giving up a Joe Mauer single and finishing with the 49th complete-game one-hitter in the last 100 years of Tiger history.

Sanchez finished the regular season with a 2.57 ERA, the best in the American League. But it was Scherzer, his teammate, who would go 21–3 and win the AL Cy Young Award. Sanchez received one first-place vote, but finished a distant fourth.

Sanchez had long proven general manager Dave Dombrowski and his scouting staff right for making the 2012 trade with the Marlins. The Tigers also got Omar Infante in the deal, filling what was a big hole at second base.

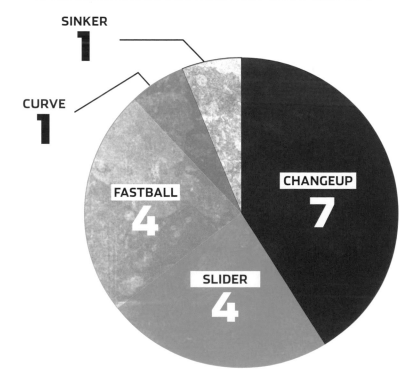

SANCHEZ'S STRIKEOUTS BY PITCH TYPE

SINKER
1

CURVE
1

FASTBALL
4

CHANGEUP
7

SLIDER
4

Dombrowski went into that July 31 deadline knowing that second base was a priority, but also believing the Tigers could use an upgrade at the back of the rotation. When scout Mike Russell recommended the deal with the Marlins, Dombrowski had one big question.

"If we get to the postseason, will he be one of our four starters?" Dombrowski asked.

Absolutely, Russell said. And that October, Sanchez had a 1.77 ERA in three postseason starts, including a win over the New York Yankees in which he allowed just three hits in seven shutout innings.

Two months later, after Sanchez had become a free agent, the Tigers would re-sign him, giving him a five-year, $80 million contract after the Chicago Cubs had made a strong bid.

"Listen, I want to be a Tiger," Sanchez told Gene Mato, his agent.

"To me, you're looking at one of the best pitchers in the league," Dombrowski said when the deal was announced. "We're looking at him to continue to grow."

Sanchez did grow. Verlander was right. He wasn't the same pitcher who once hated facing the Atlanta Braves.

He was the pitcher who could go out on a cool April night and shut the Braves down. He was the pitcher who could go out and do what no other Tiger pitcher had done, before or since.

See?

Max Scherzer Goes

21–3

in 2013

Max Scherzer arrived in Detroit with a big arm and bigger questions.

He threw hard, but he also threw with a violent motion that had some thinking he might never stay healthy. The Arizona Diamondbacks wondered whether he might need to move to the bullpen, and they weren't the only ones. When the Tigers acquired Scherzer as part of a huge three-way winter meetings deal with the Diamondbacks and New York Yankees, Scherzer was far more than a throw-in but far less than a sure-fire star.

This wasn't the same thing as Dave Dombrowski trading for Miguel Cabrera or David Price. This one took some projection.

The Tigers projected right.

The rest of the December 2009 trade would end up looking good for the Tigers. Austin Jackson first became a solid replacement for Curtis Granderson in center field, and eventually one of the key pieces needed to acquire Price. The Yankees and Diamondbacks were happy early on with their returns, as well.

But as the years went on, two things became more and more obvious. One, Max Scherzer was easily the best of the seven players in the trade. Two, Max Scherzer not only can start, he can be one of the very best starting pitchers in the game.

The proof came in 2013, and whether Scherzer likes it or not, his 21–3 record that season became part of the evidence.

"For me, if I win 20, it's a team achievement," he said repeatedly in the weeks leading up to his 20th win.

Scherzer pitched at least seven innings 14 times allowing no more than two runs.

"It would be naïve for me to take all the credit for this," he said again the night of the 20th win. "They're the ones out there playing great defense. They're the ones scoring the extra hits."

And he was the one who turned into a pitcher so good that the Tigers would offer him $144 million the following spring, and a player so confident that he would turn down that money in favor of waiting six months to become a free agent (where he would get $210 million from the Washington Nationals).

Scherzer would argue that the 21 wins (or the three losses) aren't the best way to measure his breakthrough season, and he'd be right. But the simplest of numbers are also the simplest way to show that all those people who weren't sure he could succeed as a big-league starter were wrong.

He turned into a 200-inning starter, an All-Star starter, a Cy Young winner. The modern metrics of WAR and WHIP and FIP celebrated his development, too.

But it sure didn't hurt that just about every time he pitched, the Tigers won. It didn't hurt him, and it certainly didn't hurt them.

.875 Max Scherzer
(21–3), 2013

.862 Bill Donovan
(25–4), 1907

.842 Schoolboy Rowe
(16–3), 1940

.838 Denny McLain
(31–6), 1968

.828 Justin Verlander
(24–5), 2011

He improved his curveball, and his other pitches got better. He made his delivery more consistent, and he found that when the seventh and eighth innings came around, he was still in the game. His teammates had plenty of time to score the runs he needed to win, and most often he was handing the ball off to the best pitchers in the bullpen rather than the shakiest ones.

Fourteen times that season, Scherzer pitched at least seven innings while allowing no more than two runs. In the month of May alone, he had four starts where he went eight innings.

His run support was good (5.59 per nine innings, third in the majors), but Scherzer rarely needed all the help. He won games 17–2, 10–0, and 6–1. Just to prove that he did need a little help, though, his three losses came in three games where the Tigers were held to a single run.

Of course, if you put that another way, you could say that when the Tigers scored at least two runs in a Scherzer start, he never lost.

His .875 winning percentage was the best ever for a full-time Tigers starting pitcher, and his three losses are tied for the fewest ever by any major league 20-game winner.

Whatever you think of pitchers' wins—and Scherzer is far from the only one to consider it an overrated and overused statistic—20 wins remains a milestone that most pitchers and pitching coaches strive for. If the increased use of bullpens has made it less meaningful, it's also made it harder to get. Scherzer, Justin Verlander (2011), and Bill Gullickson (1991) are the Tigers' only 20-game winners since Jack Morris left town.

They all leave eventually, but some leave with more of a legacy than others. Scherzer's legacy will be overwhelmingly positive, that of a talented pitcher who came in with questions and answered them with a Cy Young.

And with the 21–3 season that led to it.

Tiger Pitchers Strike Out

1,428

in 2013

The first out the Tigers recorded in 2013 was a Justin Verlander strikeout. There were more to come.

Many more.

Even at a time in baseball where strikeouts have become more prevalent than ever, what the Tiger pitchers did that year was extraordinary.

"Pretty incredible, really," pitching coach Jeff Jones said.

From the first day of the season (when Verlander and the bullpen combined to fan 12 Minnesota Twins) to the last (when Verlander and the bullpen combined to fan 13 Miami Marlins), Tiger pitchers averaged 8.8 strikeouts for every nine innings pitched.

That's not one guy. That's an entire 20-man pitching staff.

Nolan Ryan, the greatest strikeout pitcher of all time, averaged 9.5 strikeouts per nine innings in his career. The Tigers nearly did that as a staff.

To put it another way, just a tick under one-third of all the outs the Tigers recorded in 2013 (32.5 percent) came via a strikeout.

"It wasn't like a competition," Jones said. "But I do think each guy pushed each other."

Jones didn't even realize until the final weekend of the season that the Tigers were on a record pace. The 2003 Chicago Cubs of Kerry Wood and Mark Prior had **The Tigers were just the third team ever with 3 200-strikeout pitchers.** the old mark of 1,404. The Tigers actually topped it with nearly two games to spare, when Anibal Sanchez struck out the leadoff hitter on the next-to-last day of the season.

Sanchez had 202 strikeouts, the sixth-most in the American League but only the third-most on his own staff. Max Scherzer fanned 240, and Verlander had 217. The Tigers were just the third team ever with three 200-strikeout pitchers, joining the 1967 Minnesota Twins and the 1969 Houston Astros.

As it turned out, the Tigers only held the major league record for one year. The 2014 Indians broke it with 1,450 strikeouts.

Still, 1,428 was impressive. And it wasn't by accident.

Dave Dombrowski isn't the only general manager in baseball who favors hard-throwing pitchers (most do), but he may put as much emphasis on it as anyone. Dombrowski's scouts know that if they're ever going to turn in a pitcher with below-average velocity, they'd better be prepared to make a great case.

Velocity doesn't always equal strikeouts, but it helps. Dombrowski believes that power pitching wins in October, and power pitching does mean strikeout pitching.

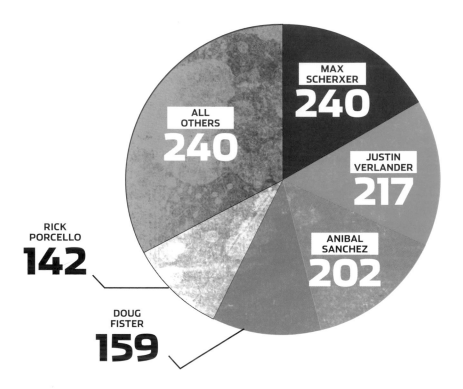

THE TIGERS' RECORD 1,428 STRIKEOUTS, BY PITCHER

MAX SCHERXER 240

ALL OTHERS 240

JUSTIN VERLANDER 217

ANIBAL SANCHEZ 202

RICK PORCELLO 142

DOUG FISTER 159

Even with that philosophy, Dombrowski's Tiger teams had never led the major leagues in strikeouts, not until 2013.

It happened that year because Verlander had his fifth straight season topping 200 strikeouts. It happened because Dombrowski's decision to acquire Scherzer as part of a three-way deal with the Arizona Diamondbacks and New York Yankees at the 2009 winter meetings had paid off big-time. The Diamondbacks weren't really sure whether Scherzer was a starter or a reliever, but with the Tigers he blossomed into a Cy Young winner with three straight 200-strikeout seasons.

It happened because when the Tigers needed help at midseason in 2012, scout Mike Russell suggested Sanchez, the sometimes brilliant but inconsistent pitcher the Miami Marlins were ready to unload. Sanchez had always been able to strike batters out, but in 2013 he did it at a higher rate than he ever had before.

It was Sanchez who turned in the 2013 staff's signature strikeout game, when he fanned 17 Atlanta Braves on April 26 to beat Mickey Lolich's team record for one game.

Before the year was over, each of the Tigers' five regular starters would have at least two double-digit strikeout games (Scherzer led the way with eight).

But it wasn't just the starters. Setup man Al Alburquerque had 70 strikeouts in just 49 innings, and closer Joaquin Benoit had 73 in 67 innings. Eight Tiger pitchers had more strikeouts than innings pitched.

It wasn't just the Tigers taking advantage of bad lineups, either. In the 11 postseason games the Tigers played against the Oakland Athletics and Boston Red Sox, their pitchers struck out 130 in 96 innings, an even higher strikeout rate than they had during the regular season.

Even in an era where hitters don't seem to mind striking out, that was quite an accomplishment.

Doyle Alexander goes

9–0

in 1987

The Tigers once traded a batting champion (Harvey Kuenn) for a home run champion (Rocky Colavito). They once traded their manager (Jimmy Dykes) for the Cleveland Indians manager (Joe Gordon). They traded for a guy who would win the Triple Crown (Miguel Cabrera) and for a guy who would win the Cy Young (Max Scherzer), and they traded for a guy who had already won the Cy Young (David Price).

But what might be the most discussed and debated trade in Tiger history was the one Bill Lajoie made on August 12, 1987.

John Smoltz for Doyle Alexander.

You like it, or you don't. The Tigers don't win the division in '87 without Alexander. But it cost them a guy headed for the Hall of Fame, a guy who helped the Atlanta Braves make the playoffs 13 times and helped them win a World Series.

John Smoltz was 4–10 with a 5.68 ERA at Double-A Glens Falls when the trade was made. He was only 20 years old and already pitching in Double-A, but there was no guarantee he would develop into a big-league pitcher, let alone into a guy who was great as a starter (213 wins) and as a closer (154 saves).

But he did.

Alexander was 5–10 with a 4.13 ERA for the Braves when the trade was made. There was no guarantee he would be the guy who pitched the Tigers into the playoffs.

But he was.

We'll never know if Smoltz would have developed the same had he remained with the Tigers. We'll never know if he alone could have helped lift the Tigers out

The Tigers won all _11_ of Alexander's starts after the trade.

of the depths of 19 years without a postseason appearance (it's doubtful).

What we do know is that Smoltz for Alexander is one of the best, and best-cited, examples of trading a chance at the future for a shot at winning now. What we also know is that in that sense, it was a deal that worked for both teams.

It's easy to say that the Tigers would have been far better off had they been able to make the Alexander trade for Steve Searcy. Searcy and Smoltz were the two young pitchers the teams discussed, but eventually it was Smoltz rather than Searcy who ended up being the price for Alexander.

In his book *Character Is Not a Statistic,* Lajoie wrote that most of the other Tiger executives liked Searcy more than Smoltz. He said he preferred Smoltz, but not strongly enough to fight the rest of the group.

Bobby Cox, then the Braves general manager, wanted Smoltz.

MOST WINS WITHOUT A LOSS, TIGERS, ONE SEASON

Doyle Alexander	Bud Thomas	Drew Smyly	Fred Gladding	Archie McKain
1987	1939	2013	1966	1940
9	7	6	5	5

Lajoie and the Tigers were trying to get another championship out of what remained from the team that won in 1984. Lajoie knew that Dan Petry was struggling, and he knew that the 36-year-old Alexander had experience winning in the American League and also had a history of pitching well in September.

The Tigers trailed the Blue Jays by 1½ games in the AL East when they made the trade. It would be a close race right to the end, with the Tigers coming out on top only because they swept the Blue Jays on the final weekend. Alexander started the first game of that weekend series, going seven innings to beat the Jays, 4–3.

It was Alexander's 11th start since the trade, and the Tigers won all 11. He averaged more than eight innings a start, and his 1.53 ERA was by far the lowest of any American League pitcher with 50 or more innings (Blue Jays closer Tom Henke was second, at 2.49).

He had three complete-game shutouts, and one game where he pitched seven scoreless innings and another where he pitched eight. His success seemed to lift the whole team, with the Tigers going 34–18 from the day they made the trade.

Up to that point, it was easy to see the trade as a great success for the Tigers. They made the deal to get to the playoffs, and Alexander got them there.

Then it all began to change.

The Tigers lost to the Minnesota Twins in the playoffs, with Alexander losing Game 1 and Game 5. Alexander's 1988 season wasn't bad, but it was nothing like '87, and the Tigers collapsed down the stretch, in a sign of things to come. He would stay around long enough to lose 18 games in 1989, his final big-league season.

That same year, John Smoltz was a 22-year-old All-Star, the first of his eight All-Star appearances. Two years later, he was pitching the Braves into the 1991 World Series, the first of five times he would get there with the Braves.

By then, Bill Lajoie had joined the Braves, too. He stepped down as Tigers GM after the 1990 season, and signed on with the Braves as a special assistant to general manager John Schuerholz.

Lajoie would help the Braves win the 1995 World Series, and later he would help the Boston Red Sox win the 2004 World Series. He would never work again as a general manager, but he would have a hand in some of baseball's biggest trades.

No one he was involved in trading for did any better than Doyle Alexander did for the Tigers. No one he was involved in trading away did any better than John Smoltz did for the Atlanta Braves.

And no deal was as discussed and debated in the years to come as that Smoltz for Alexander trade was—and still is today.

Frank Tanana's Division-Clinching

1-0

Win

He was the 17-year-old kid, clutching his left arm as he walked off the Tiger Stadium mound, wondering where life would take him. He was the 34-year-old veteran, bouncing around that same field in triumph, this time with both arms raised firmly in the air.

Frank Tanana was the Detroit kid who lived a life of contrasts: Nolan Ryan's hard-throwing and hard-partying sidekick with the California Angels of the mid-1970s, turned into a born-again Christian and a born-again pitcher when he arrived back in Detroit with the Tigers of the mid-1980s.

His 1971 appearance at Tiger Stadium, the one where he hurt his arm four innings into the Detroit Catholic League championship game, kept the Tigers and other teams from drafting him. The way the story goes, Angels scout Carl Ackerman skipped that game and got fired because of it, but the Angels got Tanana because their scout didn't have any idea he was hurt.

The 1987 game would be different, the culmination of the Tigers' comeback from the dead against the Toronto Blue Jays and the high point of Tanana's own comeback from the arm trouble that had threatened his career. It was the final day of the season, and while the Tigers had already won three straight (including two over the Blue Jays) to move into first place, they still needed one more to avoid a one-game playoff for the Eastern Division crown.

Tanana gave it to them. He got a lead on Larry Herndon's second-inning home run off Jimmy Key, and he made the one run hold up with a six-hit shutout. As Jim Palmer told him on the ABC telecast, it had to be his biggest game of the year.

"When you get to my age, every game's a big game," Tanana responded. "Because when you stink, you're done."

Tanana wasn't done, not at age 34 and not for a few years after that. He lasted eight years with his hometown team and 21 big-league seasons in all, tied with John Smoltz and behind only Jim Kaat for the most by a Michigan-born pitcher.

Tanana's 240 career wins are also second-most (also behind Jim Kaat) for a pitcher born in Michigan.

He was a star at Detroit Catholic Central, a dominating left-hander who could throw strike after strike. He was so highly regarded that the Tigers figured he'd be gone well before their first draft pick, 11th overall. All that changed on that day at Tiger Stadium, and even though Tanana was still available when they picked, the Tigers passed on him and chose Tom Veryzer instead.

Three years later, Tanana was pitching at Tiger Stadium—but for the Angels. He was only 20 years old, but he was already in his first full season in the major leagues.

He would later suffer a more serious arm injury, and lose the blazing fastball. He'd be traded to the Boston Red Sox, then sign with the Texas Rangers as a free agent. It wasn't until June 1985 that he would get the chance to come home, when the Tigers acquired him from the Rangers in a midseason deal for Duane James.

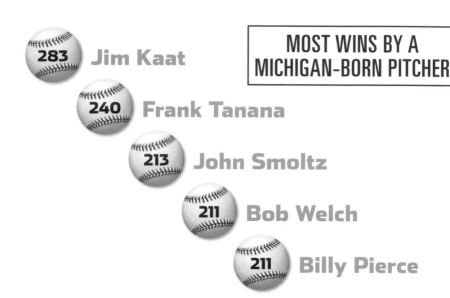

283 Jim Kaat

240 Frank Tanana

213 John Smoltz

211 Bob Welch

211 Billy Pierce

General manager Bill Lajoie had long been looking for a left-handed starter. Tanana was 2–7 with a 5.91 ERA, and his fastball could barely be called that. But Lajoie had always liked Tanana. He had even known Tanana's father when both were kids growing up in Detroit.

He offered the Rangers their pick of three younger pitchers: James, Mike Henneman, or Jeff Robinson. Lajoie hoped they would pick James, and they did.

The Tigers got Tanana. The 10 wins he had the rest of the season weren't enough to get them back to the playoffs or World Series for a second straight year, but the move would pay off in 1987. Tanana went 15–10 that year, and the 15th win was easily the biggest one.

It had already been quite a week for the Tigers, a week that had turned "bear trap" into a baseball term that would live on in Detroit.

"Maybe we're setting the biggest bear trap of all time," Kirk Gibson had said, on the Sunday before in Toronto, when the Tigers had rebounded from three straight losses but still trailed the first-place Jays by 2½ games with just a week to go.

The '87 Jays will forever be known for one of baseball's great collapses, losers of their final seven games in a race they should have put away. Jerome Holtzman of the *Chicago Tribune* compared them to the 1964 Philadelphia Phillies, the Gene Mauch team that blew a six-game lead with 12 to play.

But in Detroit, that final week—and especially that final weekend—will long be remembered more for what the Tigers did than for what the Blue Jays didn't. A Tiger team that should never have had a chance, won three consecutive one-run games against the team that was supposed to win.

The Tigers wouldn't make it back to the playoffs for another 19 years.

Doyle Alexander, perhaps the best midseason trade acquisition ever, beat the Blue Jays 4–3 on Friday night. Alan Trammell's scorching 12th-inning ground ball that got through Manny Lee gave the Tigers a 3–2 win on Saturday, putting them a game up with one to play.

And then came Tanana, whose 3.01 career ERA against Toronto was his best against any AL team other than Baltimore.

"Every time he pitches against us, I think he's Cy Young," Jesse Barfield said.

Tanana was a little shaky early, allowing the Blue Jays two baserunners in the first and avoiding big trouble in the fourth only because Lee missed a sign and got Cecil Fielder thrown out trying to steal on what was supposed to be a hit and run.

As the game went on, Tanana got tougher, making the 1–0 lead look bigger and bigger. The final out came on a Garth Iorg roller that Tanana fielded himself, and the improbable Tiger pitcher had given the improbable team a spot in the playoffs.

The 98-win Tigers went on to lose to the 85-win Minnesota Twins, who would also beat the St. Louis Cardinals to win the World Series. But the 98 wins were misleading. The Tigers really were improbable champs.

For years after 1987, Sparky Anderson would tell anyone who asked that the '87 division title was the hardest one to explain.

"Roger Craig asked me how we did it," Sparky would say. "I told him, 'Roger, I can't even begin to tell you. There isn't enough time in the world to explain that one.'"

The Tigers wouldn't make it back to the playoffs for another 19 years. Anderson would never manage another playoff game. Tanana would never pitch in one.

His career would go on, through five more seasons with the Tigers and then one final season in New York split between the Mets and the Yankees. He had 66 more wins, including three more shutouts.

He would never pitch another game like that one, on the last day of the 1987 season, when he could stand on the Tiger Stadium field and thrust his arms in the air.

Willie Hernandez Saves

32

Straight Games in 1984

The 1983 World Series was one of the most important in Tiger history.

Yes, the 1983 World Series, the one where the Baltimore Orioles beat the Philadelphia Phillies. And the one where the Tigers first came up with the idea of trading for Willie Hernandez.

Club executives would routinely attend the World Series back then, even if their team wasn't in it. It was baseball's signature event, and it was also where teams could begin laying the groundwork for winter moves.

So when the Orioles clinched the World Series in Game 5 with a 5–0 win over the Phillies, newly named Tigers general manager Bill Lajoie was there. He and manager Sparky Anderson sat in the stands at Veterans Stadium and watched Hernandez pitch three perfect innings in what was already a lost cause.

The '83 Phillies were done, but the '84 Tigers were just getting going.

"You get that guy," Anderson told Lajoie, "and we'll win the World Series."

It took five months, but Lajoie got that guy. He got Hernandez, and the Tigers won the World Series.

The Tigers won

104 games

and the World Series.

We'll never know if they could have won it without him. We'll never know if the Tigers would have traded for him, anyway, even if Anderson and Lajoie hadn't watched him pitch so well that afternoon in October.

What we do know is what happened. Lajoie traded for Hernandez with days to go in spring training, and Hernandez had one of the best seasons of any reliever in major league history. The Tigers won 104 games, and they won the World Series.

Maybe managers and GMs ought to attend the World Series every year.

Lajoie tells the story of the Hernandez trade in his book, *Character Is Not a Statistic.* He tells of the afternoon at the World Series, but also of how he nearly traded for San Francisco Giants reliever Gary Lavelle that winter instead.

Fortunately for the Tigers, the deal fell through when Lavelle wouldn't agree to a contract extension. Fortunately for the Tigers, a possible deal that would have sent Hernandez to the Toronto Blue Jays fell through, too.

Lajoie found out that the Phillies liked Glenn Wilson, an outfielder the Tigers could afford to trade because they had nowhere for him to play. He asked Sparky to have Wilson take extra batting practice before a spring training game against the Phillies in Clearwater, knowing that Wilson was a great batting-practice hitter.

Sure enough, Wilson impressed. Sure enough, the Tigers were able to get Hernandez, along with first baseman Dave Bergman, in a deal for Wilson and John Wockenfuss.

Bergman was a useful player off the bench, and would hit one of the more memorable home runs of the Tigers' 1984 season, at the end of a 13-pitch at-bat off Toronto's Roy Lee Jackson. Hernandez won both the Cy Young Award and the American League's Most Valuable Player Award.

He appeared in 80 games that year, and the Tigers won 63 of them. He was credited with 32 saves, and in 21 of those games he pitched more than one inning. He didn't have many saves early on, because when the Tigers started 35–5 they didn't play all that many close games.

But as the season went on, Hernandez became more and more important. In May, June, and July, he pitched in 39 games and saved 19 of them. In 75 innings in those three months, he had a 1.32 ERA. He was almost as good in August and September—and October.

His only regular-season blown save came on September 28, on the meaningless final weekend of the season, when he entered the game with the tying run on third and allowed a sacrifice fly. In the years to come, Sparky would say that if he realized it was a big deal to go through a season without a blown save, he never would have pitched Hernandez in that situation.

In 75 innings, he had a 1.32 ERA.

The Tigers, who had clinched the division 10 days earlier, certainly didn't need the win.

Hernandez was on the mound for the final out of the clincher, and also for the final out when the Tigers finished off their playoff sweep of the Kansas City Royals. He was on the mound for the final out of their World Series clincher against the San Diego Padres, too.

Hernandez finished the 1984 season with a 1.92 ERA, the best of his 13-year career and the best in 39 years for any Tiger pitcher with 140 or more innings. Yes, Hernandez pitched 140⅓ innings that year, the third-most ever for a pitcher with 32 or more saves.

Years later, Hernandez would tell author George Cantor that he had better stuff in other years, but that he never had better command than he did in 1984. He also figured that changing leagues was an advantage, because American League hitters had never seen the screwball he learned from Mike Cuellar and began using in 1983.

Hernandez had a good year in '83. He helped get the Phillies to the World Series, after they acquired him in a May trade with the Chicago Cubs. But he was a setup man there, because the Phillies had a good closer in Al Holland.

The Tigers didn't. Anderson and Lajoie knew they would need one, but they didn't know where they'd find him.

They went to the World Series, and they found Willie Hernandez.

And then he took them to the next World Series with him.

Jose Valverde Saves

49

Games in 2011

Jose Valverde fit right in.

First he was loved. Then he was hated.

First he set a record. Then he couldn't hold his job.

Why does it always go this way with Tiger closers?

Tiger closers and Red Wings goalies, Mike Ilitch once said. No other job in town is guaranteed to get you that much heat.

Unless you're perfect.

In 2011, Jose Valverde was just about perfect. He saved 49 games, the most in Tiger history. He had no blown saves, the first closer in Tiger history to go through a season without one.

Only Eric Gagne, who went 55 for 55 with the 2003 Los Angeles Dodgers, ever had a better save record. But really, can you be any better than perfect?

Jose Valverde skips to the mound against the Texas Rangers during Game 3 of the 2011 ALCS against the Rangers.
(*Mark Cunningham*)

Maybe not, but you sure can be worse than perfect. You can be Jose Valverde in 2012 and beyond. You can be Jose Valverde in October 2012, when his manager finally had to make the tough move of dumping his closer in the middle of a playoff series.

Valverde never lost his sense of humor, and he never lost his sense of flair. He celebrated the same, just not nearly as often. The fans just didn't appreciate it nearly as much.

We'll look back on that 2011 season with admiration. We'll look back on what happened after that with questions.

We'll wonder why it always seems to go this way with Tiger closers.

Willie Hernandez was near-perfect in 1984, one of the biggest contributors to that magical season. Willie Hernandez, or Guillermo as he eventually wanted to be called, became so hated that fans started booing the minute he emerged to begin warming up.

Mike Henneman set the club's all-time saves record. The night he set the record, he was booed on his way to the mound.

Todd Jones beat Henneman's career record, and also beat John Hiller's single-season record. He was the beloved "roller coaster," as Ernie Harwell dubbed him. Beloved, that is, until he didn't get the job done.

Jones held the job for a while. Actually, he held it twice, first from 1997 until he was traded away in July 2001 (he cried that day, even though he was leaving a losing team to join one in a pennant race), and then from 2006 to 2008, when he helped the Tigers to the World Series.

Fernando Rodney took Jones' place, but after a shaky 2009 season, the Tigers wanted someone better. They settled on Valverde, a free agent who had a 47-save season with the Arizona Diamondbacks and a 44-save season with the Houston Astros.

His first season with the Tigers was all right, but nothing special. He had 26 saves, but also three blown saves and four losses. The team finished 81–81. Valverde didn't cost the Tigers a chance at the playoffs, but he didn't really do anything to get them there, either.

The 2011 season would be different.

Valverde had five saves (and two wins) in April, when he allowed just one run in 10²/₃ innings. By June 4, he was 15 for 15. By July 31, he was 28 for 28, and the Tigers were in first place in the American League Central.

He danced around the mound after big outs, just as he had always done. The only difference in 2011 was that there were more outs to dance to.

He was bold, and he was brash. And when he was perfect, it all went over just fine with Tiger fans.

He topped Jones' single-season club record with his 43rd save, and teammates who had been the recipient of his pies in the face made sure he got one that night, too.

He finished 49 for 49, with a 2.24 ERA. He had three more saves in October, and also one more big proclamation.

After Game 2 of the Division Series against the New York Yankees, with the series tied at one win apiece, Jose Valverde declared that it was over.

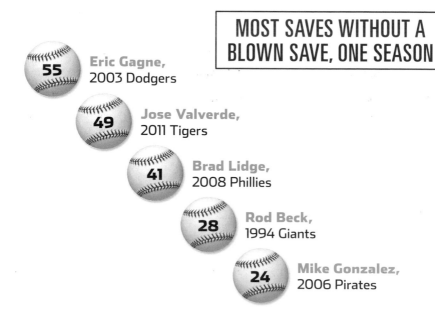

MOST SAVES WITHOUT A BLOWN SAVE, ONE SEASON

55 Eric Gagne, 2003 Dodgers

49 Jose Valverde, 2011 Tigers

41 Brad Lidge, 2008 Phillies

28 Rod Beck, 1994 Giants

24 Mike Gonzalez, 2006 Pirates

"Oh yeah," he said that day at Yankee Stadium. "It's over already. [Justin] Verlander has it [in Game 3]. Next day, have the celebration in Detroit—100 percent. The Yankees have a good team, but I think that's it for them."

He said he was joking, and then he said he wasn't. And even if his prediction didn't exactly come true, the Tigers did end up beating the Yankees—in five games, not four.

They didn't beat the Texas Rangers in the ALCS, in part because their too-thin bullpen didn't hold up. Valverde had to pitch three straight days, with multiple innings in two of the games, and in Game 4 the Rangers torched him for a four-run 11th inning.

It didn't count as a blown save. Valverde wouldn't have one of those until Opening Day 2012.

It wasn't taken as a sign that the Tigers needed to find another closer. That wouldn't happen until October 2012, when Valverde struggled against the Oakland A's and then collapsed against the Yankees. Manager Jim Leyland basically got through the rest of the ALCS without a closer, with Phil Coke more or less taking over.

Valverde would pitch again, returning to the Tigers for 20 games (and nine saves) in 2013 and pitching for the New York Mets at the beginning of 2014. But he would never be the same.

He was perfect for a year, and before long he was perfectly awful.

Why does it always go this way with Tiger closers?

John Hiller Saves

38

Games in 1973

John Hiller set one record that wasn't broken for 10 years, and another one that wasn't broken for 13.

And then there was the unofficial record he set, the one that may never be broken.

How many guys lead the league in saves after suffering a heart attack?

Not just a minor heart attack, either, if there is such a thing. When Hiller's heart temporarily gave out in January 1971, he was in the hospital for five weeks.

"I kept asking them when I could pitch again," he said once he had recovered—and once he had pitched again for the Tigers.

It's quite a story, and would have been even if Hiller hadn't come all the way back to break the major league record with a 38-save season in 1973. Dan Quisenberry of the Kansas City Royals broke

Hiller's single-season record in 1983, but his Tiger career record of 125 lasted into the 1990s, when Mike Henneman finally topped it.

Hiller still holds the Tigers record for most career appearances, but it really is amazing that after 1971 he had any appearances at all.

He missed that entire season, and even went back to the hospital for surgery to remove seven feet of his intestines, a treatment that doctors believed could allow him to return to pitching. He had to visit multiple doctors the next winter, just to get permission to join the Tigers in spring training.

... appeared in 65 games, including pitching nine times in the first 15 days of September.

Even then, they brought him back only as a minor-league instructor. It wasn't until late May that he came back to Detroit to pitch batting practice, and not until July that manager Billy Martin decided to put him in a game.

Amazingly, Hiller pitched so well that he became a key part of a team that made the playoffs. He appeared in three of the five playoff games against Oakland, and even got credit for one of the two Tiger wins.

The next year, he saved 38 games. In an age before pitchers were designated as one-inning closers, Hiller got four or more outs in 22 of his 38 saves.

His ERA that year: 1.44. He appeared in 65 games, including pitching nine times in 15 days at the start of September. He finished fourth in Cy Young voting and fourth in MVP voting, and he was an easy choice for Comeback Player of the Year.

He was 30 years old. He was also just 2½ years removed from having a heart attack.

Hiller said later that when he got out of the hospital after surgery, he found his weight had dropped from 220 pounds all the way down to 150. He said his legs were so weak that he couldn't even walk one hole on a golf course.

MOST GAMES PITCHED, TIGERS CAREER

 John Hiller **545**

 Hooks Dauss **538**

 Mickey Lolich **508**

 Dizzy Trout **493**

 Mike Henneman **491**

He got a job selling furniture, and also worked out three hours a day to build his strength back. He said that by spring training 1972, he was throwing as hard as he ever had.

It took some doing to convince the Tigers, who were especially cautious because of the recent memory of Chuck Hughes dying on the Tiger Stadium field while playing for the NFL's Detroit Lions. But Hiller credited Dr. Clarence Livingood, the Tigers' longtime physician, with championing his cause.

"He ended up releasing a national statement that said, 'John Hiller will have a heart attack if you keep him away from baseball before he'll ever have one on the ballfield,'" Hiller told an interviewer in 2006.

In later years, Hiller maintained that the heart attack made him better, as a person and as a pitcher.

"I learned what was important in life," he once said. "I always wanted to pitch well. But I also learned baseball is a game. As a stopper, sometimes you're going to get them, and sometimes they're going to get you. If they get you, you have to get over it fast.

"The next night might belong to you."

It was a philosophy that took Hiller all the way to the Canadian Baseball Hall of Fame.

In 1971, his heart nearly got him. But the rest of his career, and the rest of his life, belonged to him.

Joel Zumaya Throws a

105

mph Fastball

Watching Joel Zumaya pitch was always a two-step process.

Step 1: Watch the pitch.

Step 2: Watch the radar gun.

You wanted to see the overmatched batter swing and miss. You also wanted to see 100.

Or 101, or perhaps even 102.

One day, it was even 105!

Actually, it was 104.8 mph, according to MLB.com's GameDay. It was in the 2006 playoffs, Game 1 of the ALCS in Oakland, a fastball that Frank Thomas took for ball two. It's hard to know how accurate a reading it was, because these were the very early days of MLB.com's Pitchf/x system. On many pitches in that same game, there was no velocity reading at all.

There's no question it was fast. It might even have been 105.

Zumaya came to the Tigers at a time when radar readings were more accessible than ever, but not yet free from variation and even outright manipulation. One American League general manager later admitted to me that he had instructed his staff never to post a gun reading higher than 95 mph when Zumaya was on the mound, no matter how hard the actual pitch was.

Tiger players accused the St. Louis Cardinals of pulling the same shenanigans in the 2006 World Series, when the Zumaya gun readings shown on the Busch Stadium scoreboard didn't match up with the ones shown on the Fox telecast. The thought was that lower gun readings could get into Zumaya's head, since he regularly checked the board after throwing a pitch and might try to overthrow the next one if he thought his velocity was down.

No matter what anyone tried, it was obvious that Zumaya was throwing harder than everyone else. *The Bill James Handbook*

MOST TRIPLE-DIGIT FASTBALLS, 2006

233 Joel Zumaya

26 Kyle Farnsworth

19 Justin Verlander

7 Felix Hernandez

Source: *The Bill James Handbook,* 2007

Joel Zumaya goes for triple digits in a 2006 game against the Tampa Bay Devil Rays. *(A. Messerschmidt)*

said Zumaya threw 233 pitches that season clocked over 100 mph. No other pitcher in baseball had more than Kyle Farnsworth's 26, and the only other pitcher in double-digits on triple-digit pitches was Justin Verlander, with 19.

Baseball Info Solutions listed Zumaya's best pitch of the season at 104 mph. No one else threw a pitch above 102.

"If I was up there hitting against a guy like me, I'd be scared," Zumaya said that season.

The Pitchf/x system became operational everywhere starting in 2007, and that year Zumaya's average fastball was clocked at 97.6 mph, the fastest of any reliever in baseball. His 2008 average of 98.42 was also the fastest. And in 2009, the system had him with an MLB-best average of 100.05 mph.

Zumaya's average fastball, for all the years Pitchf/x has been in operation, was 99.27. Even now, that ranks him just behind Aroldis Chapman (99.45) for the best the system has seen.

The point is, he threw hard. He knew it, batters knew it, and because gun readings were more accessible than ever, we could all see it and talk about it.

And we loved it.

It's too bad it didn't last.

Zumaya was only 21 years old when he made the Tigers as a surprise rookie in spring training 2006. He was only 25 when he pitched in what turned out to be his final big-league game, in June 2010.

We may never know for sure why he couldn't stay healthy, whether it was the violent motion that allowed him to throw the ball so hard or just bad luck or maybe even video games.

Yes, video games, because when wrist and forearm problems sidelined Zumaya during those 2006 playoffs (just after the game where he was clocked at 105), Tigers general manager Dave Dombrowski said the team believed he got hurt because he spent too much time playing Guitar Hero.

Then there was the horrific scene the following May, when Zumaya walked in from the bullpen screaming in pain and grabbing his right middle finger. He had ruptured a tendon while throwing a warmup pitch, and he wouldn't appear in another major league game for three months.

A year later, he felt a "pop" in his right shoulder while moving boxes in his San Diego home. The year after that, he fractured his right elbow, and had to have a screw inserted in it. Then came Tommy John surgery.

"I want to say I feel terrible, because each time I say I feel good, I end up hurt," Zumaya said at one point when he was between injuries.

He never did make it back to what he was as a rookie. He barely made it back at all.

Finally, just before spring training opened in 2014, Joel Zumaya announced his retirement. He was only 29 years old.

His entire career had spanned just 209$\frac{2}{3}$ innings, plus six more in that 2006 postseason. He never made as much as $1 million in any season, at a time when that was below the major league average. He retired with just 13 career wins, and just five career saves.

Those numbers hardly do him justice, because anybody who saw Joel Zumaya pitch—especially in that magical 2006 season—would tell you that it was something they'll never forget.

There was a buzz when he would burst out of the Comerica Park bullpen, with Jimi Hendrix's "Voodoo Child" blaring on the sound system, and there were oohs and ahs when he threw a pitch. There was a moment to pause, a look at the board with the radar reading, and then there was another even louder reaction.

With Joel Zumaya, watching the gun could be just as much fun as watching the pitch.

Comerica Park's

36

Degree Opening Day

The first idea was to replace Tiger Stadium with a domed stadium, and if you've ever been to a baseball game in Detroit in early April, you surely understand why. So the idea was to build a dome, down by the river, 52,000 seats for baseball, 60,000 for football.

It was going to be ready in 1975.

There were models. There were drawings. There was even a signed lease.

And 20 years later, the Tigers were still playing at a rapidly deteriorating (but still venerable) Tiger Stadium, still searching for a way to get out. Eventually, they made the deal to build what became Comerica Park, which is far better than that dome was ever going to be—with one very significant exception.

It gets cold.

If you were there the day the beautiful new park opened in April 2000, you know that all too well. For all the views of downtown Detroit and all the fresh air and real grass, on that day you really wouldn't have minded a roof.

Comerica Park doesn't have one. They thought about it, even had some early designs that would have allowed for a rolling retractable roof, but Comerica Park was already expensive enough, and no one was going to spend more money to roof it.

36 *windy and drizzly* **degrees at gametime on April 11, 2000**

That's fine, as long as it doesn't rain...or snow. That's fine, as long as the temperature doesn't drop below 50 degrees... or below 40.

It was 36 degrees at gametime on April 11, 2000—36 cold and windy and drizzly degrees. It was the kind of day that ballgames get called off, except this one couldn't be.

This one had to be played.

Normally in Detroit, and in other cold-weather cities, baseball sets up a schedule where the home opener is followed by an off day. The idea is that if the weather is bad, you can move Opening Day back 24 hours, and everyone who bought a ticket for the opener still has a ticket for the opener.

The problem in 2000 was that the Seattle Mariners were the opponents, and they were traveling to Detroit after a Sunday game on the West Coast. If the Tigers wanted to play on Monday and have Tuesday as a rain date, then the Monday game was going to have to be played at night.

Opening Day at Comerica Park was not going to be a night game. So instead of playing on a Monday with the possibility of shifting it to Tuesday, the Tigers opted to play on Tuesday with no safety net. They had to play, or they were going to have a mess, with a whole bunch of people who thought they had tickets for Opening Day suddenly needing to scramble to find tickets for Game 2.

So they ignored the cold and they ignored the wind and they ignored the drizzle that may have even changed to snow or sleet at some point.

"When we went out to warm up, there was ice on the grass," Mariners catcher Dan Wilson said. "This was the worst ever."

Not for the Tigers, and not for the people of Detroit who were happy with their beautiful and comfortable new ballpark.

"The New House," *Free Press* columnist Mitch Albom wrote. "It is spectacular."

It wasn't Tiger Stadium, which was a good thing and a bad thing. You missed the intimacy and tradition of the old place, but you loved the comfort and look of the new one.

Even with a capacity a few thousand smaller than they had at Michigan and Trumbull, the Tigers drew 400,000 more fans in the first year at the new park than they had in the last year at the old one.

A few years later, when the team got better, they even drew 3 million for the first time in franchise history—and then did it three more times.

They played on days when the weather was spectacular, and on a few where it was something less.

They never played on another day like April 11, 2000. The Tigers won the game that day, 5–2. Brian Moehler got the win, Freddy Garcia the loss. Seattle's John Olerud got the first hit. Gregg Jefferies drove in the first run.

But ask anyone who was there. There's a good chance they don't remember the game.

There's no chance they don't remember the cold.

Tiger Stadium's

*440**

Foot Center Field

It wasn't 440.

You remember it as 440. It said 440. It looked like 440.

But it wasn't.

The center-field fence at Tiger Stadium was a long way from home plate. It just wasn't 440 feet away.

Not even close.

Sorry about that.

"I'm sure somebody thought it was right when they first put it up there," John McHale said.

But it wasn't right, and when the Tigers had every part of the Tiger Stadium field measured properly in the late 1990s, while they were working on a design for what would be Comerica Park, they found that all the distances on the outfield fences were wrong.

Most were close to being right, "close enough for baseball," as McHale put it in a conversation years later. The most famous one of all, the 440-foot sign in center field, was not.

The actual distance to center field at Tiger Stadium? McHale doesn't remember the exact number, but it was right around 420 feet. That's the number on the center-field fence at Comerica.

That number, we're almost certain, is right.

McHale was brought in as Tigers president in 1995. His first job was to deal with the lockout, replacement players, and Sparky Anderson's refusal to manage them, but his most important job was to get a new stadium built. As much as everyone loved Tiger Stadium, it was crumbling, attendance was sagging, and renovating it into a building that could generate the revenues needed today just wasn't going to be practical.

Looking back, McHale said he has no problem with those who fought to save it.

"You don't get the fight about the preservation of Tiger Stadium if you're not in a community that cares about its baseball team," he said.

Tiger fans do care, and many of them cared so deeply about the old ballpark that they had trouble at first embracing the new one. Comerica opened in 2000, and it grew on them as the years went by. While it may not win many rankings as baseball's best ballpark, you no longer hear any negative reviews, either.

The idea to have a concourse where fans could go to the concession stand without losing view of the field (owner Mike Ilitch's idea, McHale said) was adopted in many ballparks that followed Comerica. The large lower deck kept the park from being anywhere near as intimate as Tiger Stadium, but it also meant not as many fans were forced into nosebleed territory, a problem in most new parks.

The Tigers intentionally didn't try to reproduce Tiger Stadium, realizing that trying to do that and also provide modern conveniences made for a combination bound to fail. The one concession to that history was a flagpole in the field of play, a

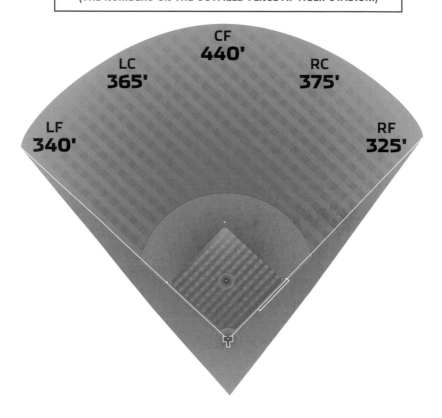

TIGER DIMENSIONS
(THE NUMBERS ON THE OUTFIELD FENCE AT TIGER STADIUM)

CF
440'

LC
365'

RC
375'

LF
340'

RF
325'

decision McHale now considers to have been a mistake (and one that didn't last when the dimensions were adjusted in 2003).

Comerica's original dimensions drew criticism almost from the start. Left field was massive, left-center was beyond the reach of even big power hitters, and it didn't help that the Tigers celebrated the change in ballparks by trading for right-handed slugger Juan Gonzalez. Gonzalez had a miserable one-year Tiger career, and after one of his drives failed to clear the fence, he turned to reporters after the game and said, "Horse[bleep] ballpark."

Other Tiger hitters, more creatively, took to referring to it as "Comerica National Park."

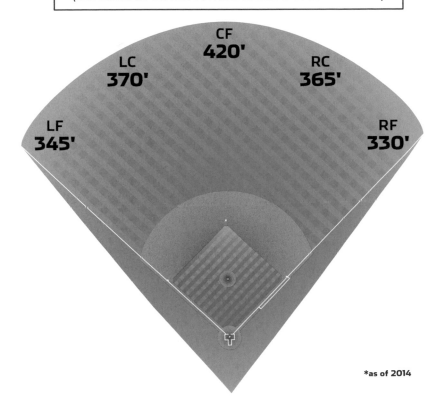

TIGER DIMENSIONS
(THE NUMBERS ON THE OUTFIELD FENCE AT COMERICA PARK*)

CF
420'

LC
370'

RC
365'

LF
345'

RF
330'

*as of 2014

McHale said the decision on the original dimensions came from the team's baseball staff, and resulted in part from the thought that the Tigers would never be among baseball's big spenders. They didn't think they would ever be able to afford big power hitters, and they had watched pitching staffs crumble when they tried to deal with Tiger Stadium's short power allies and right-field overhang.

"We tried to design a park that allowed the pitcher somewhere to go to get an out," McHale said.

Pitchers who were successful at Tiger Stadium believed they had somewhere to go when they pitched there. Keep the ball in the middle of the field, they told themselves, because it's 440 feet to center field.

It wasn't 440. It may never have been 440, although one thing many people don't realize is that the Tiger Stadium dimensions changed regularly over the first 32 years the Tigers played there.

According to records on Baseball Almanac, center field at Tiger Stadium was 467 feet when it opened in 1912. It then moved to 455 in 1930, 464 in 1931, 459 in 1936, 450 in 1937, 420 in 1942, and 440 from 1944 on.

Except we know now that it wasn't 440. The Tiger front office knew it a few years before Tiger Stadium closed, but they decided that tradition trumped accuracy when it came to signs on outfield fences.

"Somebody suggested we should paint it out and just put 'a heck of a long way,'" McHale said.

It was a heck of a long way.

It just wasn't 440.

Cecil Fielder Hits

51

Home Runs in 1990

Jerry Walker has had a distinguished career as a major league scout, helping to build playoff teams with four different organizations over a scouting career that has spanned five decades.

But the mission Tigers general manager Bill Lajoie sent him on in January 1990 didn't require a radar gun or a stopwatch.

The Tigers were coming off a 103-loss season, one so bad that it prompted club president Jim Campbell to hold his nose and tell Lajoie to enter the free-agent market with something approaching an open wallet. Lajoie signed Lloyd Moseby and Tony Phillips, but he also wanted a first baseman and had struck out on attempts to sign Kent Hrbek and Pete O'Brien.

Oh well, there was always Cecil Fielder.

Fielder had gone to Japan the year before to revive his career, and he'd hit 38 home runs in just 384 at-bats with the Hanshin Tigers. He seemed like a reasonable gamble for the two-year, $3 million contract he would cost, but the Tigers had heard some talk that he had some sort of injury.

Lajoie sent Walker to Arlington, Texas, to investigate.

"Bill just wanted to make sure that health-wise, he was okay," Walker said years later. "So I just went to his house to make sure he didn't have a broken arm or anything. He was very outgoing and friendly, but while I was there, his wife called. He said, 'Yeah, he's here, but he didn't bring a bucket of money.'"

He brought enough. Fielder proved to be one of the biggest bargains the Tigers ever signed, and provided Tiger fans with one of the most exciting seasons a sub-.500 team could ever have.

It may not sound like much today, but in 1990, a 51-homer season was huge news.

From the Sunday in early May when Fielder had a three-homer game in Toronto, and especially from the day exactly a month later when he had another three-homer game in Cleveland, reporters were coming to Tiger Stadium from everywhere to see the man billed as Michigan's first-ever popular Japanese import.

No one had hit 50 home runs in a season since George Foster did it for the Reds 13 years before. No one had done it in the American League since Roger Maris, and no one had done it for the Tigers since Hank Greenberg. Only 10 players in the history of the game had done it before Fielder made his run in 1990.

People were asking whether Fielder could make a run at Maris' record of 61, but even the run for 50 was one of the biggest baseball stories of the summer.

"It's crazy now," Fielder told reporters in September. "Every time I come to the plate, people scream for me to hit a homer."

It got crazier as the days ran out. Fielder kept up a pretty steady pace all season—he hit at least seven home runs in each month, and never more than 11—but the closer he got to 50, the more the pressure built. Fielder hit his 40th home run on August 25, the same day he became the first Tiger ever to clear Tiger Stadium's

Cecil Fielder watches one go.
(John Reid III)

left-field roof (inspiring the great *Detroit News* headline, "Fielder on the Roof").

He hit his 47th on September 16, in the Tigers' 148th game of the season. But then he hit only one home run in the next seven games. He got to 49 with six games to go, but wasn't able to hit 50 in the three remaining games at home, or in the first two games of the Tigers' final series at Yankee Stadium.

Manager Sparky Anderson, who batted Fielder second in the final two games in an effort to get him more plate appearances, said his slugger looked "over-excited."

Fielder, running out of things to say and tiring of the same questions every day, told reporters that he couldn't wait for the season to end.

"Everyone wants to see what Cec is going to do," he said. "Everyone is looking for it to happen, but Cec's brain is hurting a little right now."

But it did happen, and it was worth the wait.

In the fourth inning of the Tigers' final game, Fielder lifted a majestic shot off Steve Adkins into Yankee Stadium's upper deck. He celebrated, his teammates celebrated, and even the Yankee fans celebrated.

How many times can you ever remember a visiting player taking a curtain call in New York?

The fans insisted Cecil Fielder give them one, and he did.

"It looked like 1,000 pounds came off his back," Yankees first baseman Don Mattingly said.

"It felt like the World Series to me," said Phillips, running (and then jumping) at first base when Fielder hit No. 50. "It was just like Roger Maris the last day of the season."

It wasn't just like Maris, but for Fielder and the Tigers, it was close enough. He homered again four innings later off Alan Mills, and

MOST HOME RUNS BY A TIGER, ONE SEASON

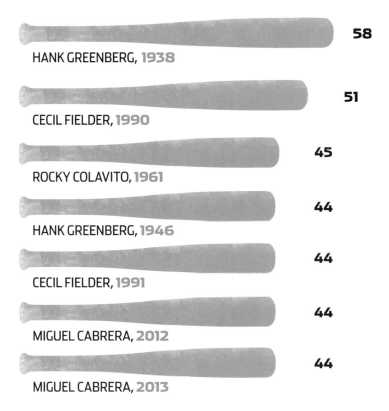

58
HANK GREENBERG, 1938

51
CECIL FIELDER, 1990

45
ROCKY COLAVITO, 1961

44
HANK GREENBERG, 1946

44
CECIL FIELDER, 1991

44
MIGUEL CABRERA, 2012

44
MIGUEL CABRERA, 2013

his 51 home runs still stand as the most by any Tiger other than Greenberg.

The Tigers had quite a bargain for their $3 million, especially when Fielder came back in 1991 with 44 homers and 133 RBIs, and a second straight second-place finish in American League MVP voting. Fielder had made quite a comeback to the major leagues, and quite a jump after being used by the Toronto Blue Jays as a platoon player.

"I am so juiced right now," Fielder said, before juiced would take on a different and much less positive meaning. "We'll probably be giving high-fives in the living room when I get home."

Eventually the Tigers did give Fielder buckets of money, at least by the standards of the time. In January 1993, he signed a five-year, $36 million deal that made him the highest paid player in the game. (It was, however, nowhere near as big as the $214 million deal the Tigers would give his son Prince 19 years later.)

Fielder's Tiger career wasn't long—he was traded to the Yankees at midseason 1996, and helped New York win the World Series that October—but his 245 home runs were more than any Tiger hit between Al Kaline's retirement in 1974 and Miguel Cabrera's arrival in 2008.

Way back in the spring of 1990, when Fielder was still something of an unknown, he hit three home runs in an exhibition game against the St. Louis Cardinals.

"He looked like King Kong today," Cardinals catcher Tom Pagnozzi told the *St. Louis Post-Dispatch.* "He was King Kong. You think Sparky Anderson will have him in the Hall of Fame tomorrow?"

Fielder never did make the Hall of Fame, not Sparky's and not the one in Cooperstown. He did give his manager and Tiger fans one of the most enjoyable seasons a 79–83 team could ever have.

Mark Fidrych's

2.34

ERA in 1976

Players sell tickets, but usually just in the sense that better players mean better teams, and better teams draw better crowds.

The 1976 Tigers weren't a good team, but every fourth or fifth day, attendance soared in a way rarely if ever seen, before or since. They'd have days and days of crowds in the 25,000–30,000 range, and then they'd have one game that drew 51,822—on a Tuesday night, against another sub-.500 team.

Mark Fidrych did that.

The Tigers have had better pitchers. They've had pitchers who have had better seasons, although Fidrych was very good in that magical summer of '76.

What the Tigers haven't had—what perhaps no major league team has ever had—is another pitcher who excited people the way Mark Fidrych did that season.

He was 21 years old. He had a great nickname. He talked to the ball. He got down on his hands and knees to landscape the mound. His games were over in two hours. He ran to the mound, raced through an inning and ran back. He was always moving. The ball was always moving. He made the major league minimum of $16,500 and drove a Dodge Colt, and his mother told the *New York Times* he was "sweating out the payments."

Detroit couldn't get enough of him. America couldn't get enough of him.

Fidrych games were over in 2 hours.

"This young man is the hope of baseball," Twins owner Calvin Griffith said.

He was a 10th-round draft pick in 1974, a 6'1" high school outfielder from western Massachusetts who rarely pitched. Tigers area scout Joe Cusick stumbled on him when he went to scout another player. Fidrych came out of the outfield to pitch in relief, and Cusick saw something he liked.

Cusick convinced Bill Lajoie to draft Fidrych, then signed him for just a $3,000 bonus.

Less than two years later, "the Bird" was a sensation, and the extra gate from even one of his starts would more than repay that $3,000 gamble.

Fidrych began the season in the bullpen, making the team out of spring training as the 25th man on the roster. He made his first big-league start on May 15 at Tiger Stadium (before only 14,583 on a Saturday afternoon), and threw a complete-game two-hitter to beat the Cleveland Indians. He went the distance in his next five starts, as well, twice pitching 11-inning complete games.

By June 28, Fidrych was 7–1 with a 2.18 ERA, and starting against the New York Yankees at Tiger Stadium in a Monday night game carried nationally by ABC. America tuned in, and 47,855 Tiger fans

MARK FIDRYCH'S
BIGGEST TIGER STADIUM CROWDS

52,528: 4/7/78 vs. Blue Jays

51,822: 8/17/76 vs. Angels

51,745: 6/29/77 vs. Red Sox

51,041: 7/9/76 vs. Royals

51,032: 7/3/76 vs. Orioles

48,361: 8/12/80 vs. Red Sox

47,855: 6/28/76 vs. Yankees

showed up to yell "Go Bird Go!" and watch another quick (1:51) complete-game win that lowered Fidrych's ERA to 2.05.

"I just throw as hard as I can and as fast as I can," Fidrych told reporters that night. "I'm kind of surprised at my success in the majors. I didn't have any idea this was going to happen."

It kept happening.

His next start drew 51,032, and this time Fidrych shut out the Baltimore Orioles. Then it was 51,041 for the start after that, a 1–0 complete-game loss to Dennis Leonard and the Kansas City Royals.

Mind you, these weren't normal crowds for the 1976 Tigers. The start against the Orioles was on a Saturday. The game the next day drew just 14,454. The start against the Royals was on a Friday. The game the next day drew just 27,630.

BEST ERA, TIGER ROOKIE

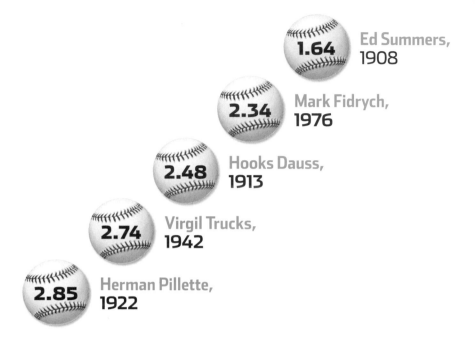

1.64 Ed Summers, 1908

2.34 Mark Fidrych, 1976

2.48 Hooks Dauss, 1913

2.74 Virgil Trucks, 1942

2.85 Herman Pillette, 1922

Fidrych started 18 home games that year, and in those 18 games the Tigers drew 605,677, more than 41 percent of their total home attendance for the season. They averaged 33,648 fans for Fidrych starts, and 15,111 for the games he didn't start.

Fidrych won 19 games. His 2.34 ERA was the American League's best, and was the best by a Tiger rookie in 68 years. It's still the second-best by a Tiger rookie, bested only by Ed Summers' 1.64 in 1908.

In 38 years since then, only two pitchers (Dave Righetti with the 1981 Yankees and Jose Fernandez with the 2013 Miami Marlins) have had a lower ERA as a rookie. No rookie since Fidrych has won an ERA title.

And no other rookie since World War II has matched Fidrych's 24 complete games.

Heck, no Tiger since Fidrych—rookie or otherwise—has matched Fidrych for complete games.

Fidrych started the All-Star Game. He won the Rookie of the Year, finished second in Cy Young voting, and even received one first-place vote for MVP (he finished 11th).

Then, just as suddenly as he became a sensation, Fidrych was history. He hurt his knee in spring training 1977. He changed his delivery, and it led to shoulder trouble.

He still made the All-Star team. He still gave the Tigers a big attendance boost the night he made his injury-delayed season debut.

But it wasn't the same. It wouldn't ever be the same. Fidrych started just 27 major league games after 1976 (spread over four seasons). He won only 10 more games after that rookie year.

He couldn't get out of the first inning against the Toronto Blue Jays on a Wednesday night in September 1980.

The crowd at Tiger Stadium that night, in what turned out to be Fidrych's last-ever home start, was just 7,129.

It was one of the Tigers' smallest crowds of the season.

Schoolboy Rowe's

16

Straight Wins

When we think of the great Tiger teams of the 1930s, we think of Mickey Cochrane and we think of Gehringer and Greenberg.

For a few months in 1934, Schoolboy Rowe was as big a star as any of them. He was a kid with a great nickname and a better fastball. He talked to the fans, and he talked to the baseball.

He was the Mark Fidrych of his day, with one important difference. The Bird was great when the Tigers weren't. The Schoolboy showed up when the Tigers were ready to win.

He pitched the Tigers into first place in early June of 1934. Nine days later, he did it again, beginning a personal winning streak that wouldn't end until late August.

Rowe won 16 straight decisions, equaling an American League record and capturing the attention of fans all around baseball. When he started in Boston, the Red Sox had their biggest midweek crowd of the season. When he started in Philadelphia, going for a 17th straight win, the Athletics had to turn fans away from an already packed Shibe Park.

The Tigers gave him a 2–0 first-inning lead, continuing a pattern that had held for months. Rowe had a 2.86 ERA during his win streak. But he also benefitted from a Tiger team that scored plenty of runs. The Tigers reached double-digits in six of his wins, and also got him a no-decision a couple of times when he wasn't sharp.

They scored five times that day in Philadelphia, but Rowe allowed 11 runs in 6²/₃ innings, the Tigers lost 13–5, and the streak was over. Rowe had to settle for tying the American League record, which had been set by Walter Johnson and equaled by Smoky Joe Wood and Lefty Grove.

Schoolboy Rowe had a **2.86 ERA** *during his win streak.*

Johnson, Wood, and Grove were huge names, and Rowe was still just a kid. Newspapers at the time referred to him as a 22-year-old, although records now show that he was actually 24.

Either way, he was in his first full season in the big leagues, and he was the biggest story going.

Gehringer later said that the newspapers drove Rowe crazy. They called him at the team hotel, and reporters sometimes even visited him there.

"Interviews, telegrams, telephone calls, autograph requests came en masse," Cochrane wrote. "I doubt if he got three hours sleep the night before the game [in Philadelphia]."

Fans came to the Tiger dugout before the game, looking for Rowe. Some wanted autographs. Others wanted more.

"A couple of feminine admirers even came into the masculine sanctity of the dugout," Cochrane wrote.

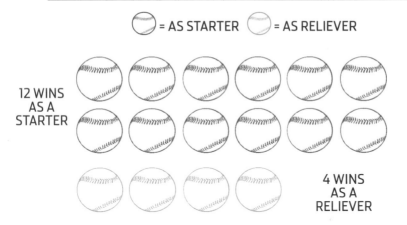

SCHOOLBOY ROWE'S 16 STRAIGHT WINS

⚾ = AS STARTER ⚾ = AS RELIEVER

12 WINS AS A STARTER

4 WINS AS A RELIEVER

Cochrane was relieved that the streak was over. The Tigers had gone 53–22 since Rowe's last loss, but they still led the second-place Yankees by just five games with a month to play.

The Tigers would hold on, winning their first pennant in 25 years. They lost to the Cardinals in the World Series, but came back the next year to beat the Chicago Cubs for the city's first championship.

Rowe, a 24-game winner in 1934, went 19–13 in 1935 and 19–10 in 1936. He hurt his arm in 1937, came back as a control pitcher, and stayed in Detroit until 1941, when the Tigers sold him to the Brooklyn Dodgers for $15,000.

He never did match the magic of those few months in 1934, the winning streak that began in June in Boston and continued through 15 starts and nine relief appearances.

"I eat a lot of vittles, climb that mound, wrap my fingers around the old baseball and say to it, 'Edna honey, let's go,'" Rowe explained during the streak.

Edna was the name of Rowe's fiancée, a name he blurted out in a radio interview after a win over the Yankees, and one opponents would yell to taunt him from then on.

The pressure built as the streak went on, but Rowe didn't crack. He threw a three-hit shutout at Yankee Stadium for the 14th straight win, with 11 strikeouts. He beat the Red Sox with another complete game to make it 15 in a row, setting up the August 25 game in Washington where he would try to tie the record.

It wasn't easy, even though Rowe pitched very well. The Tigers trailed 2–1 until the ninth, when Hank Greenberg's long three-run home run gave Rowe a 4–2 lead. Rowe needed to retire the Senators in the bottom of the ninth, and also needed to survive a rainstorm that threatened to end the game and (under the rules of the day) wipe out Greenberg's home run and give Washington the win.

The light was fading by then. Cochrane later wrote that lights were turned on in the back of the grandstand "to avoid injury to the spectators, in case there was a rush for shelter."

The Senators had the tying runs on base with two out, but Rowe got a game-ending strikeout, just before the rain came pouring down.

Rowe had his record. He would long be known for the 16 straight wins, almost as much as for the nickname he was given when he pitched for a semipro team when he was just 15 years old.

"Beaten by a schoolboy," his semipro teammates would yell at opponents when young Rowe would win a game.

In the summer of '34, plenty of American Leaguers were beaten by Schoolboy.

Other AL pitchers since have won 16 straight, and even more. But in all the years since 1934, no Tiger has ever equaled Schoolboy's streak.

Denny McLain's

31

Win Season

The biggest misconception about Denny McLain's 31-win season is that it was simply the product of a different era in baseball. No pitcher since 1968 has won 30 games in a season because so much has changed, from the move from four-man to five-man rotations, to pitch counts, and the increased use and importance of bullpens.

That's all true, but it leaves something out, something that makes McLain's accomplishment seem less impressive that it actually was.

Pitchers didn't win 30 games in the 1960s, either. Or in the 1940s or the 1950s.

In fact, as McLain was going for his 30th win in September 1968, Dizzy Dean flew in for the occasion, because at the time he was baseball's only living 30-game winner. Dean was 58 years old at the time, only 12 years younger than McLain is now. In 1968, his 30-win season was already 34 years in the past.

Before McLain, the last pitcher to win even 29 games in a season was the Tigers' Hal Newhouser, in 1944, the first of his back-to-back MVP seasons.

For that matter, Dean's big year was "only" a 30-win season, not the 31 that McLain would win. If you want to find the last 31-game winner before McLain, you have to go back another three seasons, to Lefty Grove in 1931.

Since the end of the dead-ball era, McLain and Grove are baseball's only 31-game winners.

It isn't just hard to believe (and almost impossible to accomplish) now. It was hard to believe (and almost impossible to accomplish) then, when McLain did it.

One thing that definitely was different in McLain's time: Pitchers' wins were a more respected statistic, and a more meaningful one. McLain completed an amazing 28 of his 31 wins, so he wasn't relying on relievers for help. McLain threw six shutouts and had 16 other wins where he allowed one run or two, so he didn't need all that much help from his hitters, either.

In fact, with a little more help, McLain would have won more than 31 games. He had five starts that season in which he gave up no more than two runs and still didn't get credit for a win.

And while some would no doubt say that the pressure and attention on a pitcher would be worse in today's ultra-connected world, the fact is that McLain craved the attention. He had his problems with teammates, with managers and management, and later in life with the law, but Denny McLain never feared the spotlight.

DENNY McLAIN'S 31 WINS BY MONTH

2	6	6	7	5	5
April	May	June	July	August	September

Denny McLain pitches against the Yankees at Tiger Stadium on September 19, 1968, in what would be his 31st win of the season. *(Bruce Bennett Studios/ Getty Images)*

"In 1961, Roger Maris found the media attention to be a nightmare and ran from it whenever he could," McLain wrote in his 2007 book, *I Told You I Wasn't Perfect.* "For me, it was a drug. Not only was I swarmed by writers wherever I went, but I also had magazine writers traveling with us and in my face for three straight weeks.

"It was heaven!"

Denny is different. Always has been, sometimes for better, sometimes for worse.

As a player, he got suspended for gambling, and also for misbehaving. As an ex-player, he made a mess of his life, twice ending up in prison.

On the field, though, McLain could do things others couldn't. He threw a 229-pitch complete game in 1966, with nine walks and 11 strikeouts. He was a 20-game winner that year, even though he led the league in earned runs and home runs allowed (42, in 38 starts).

He gave up home runs in 1967, too (a league-leading 35 that year), and even in his amazing 1968 season. McLain led the league by giving up 31 homers, but gave up so few other big hits that he allowed just 73 earned runs and finished with a 1.96 ERA, fourth-best in the American League in that pitching-dominated season.

The Tigers had tried to trade McLain the winter before, but were more than fortunate that they couldn't. McLain later said that he strengthened his right side by bowling all winter.

"I loved the 10th frame like I loved the ninth inning," he would write in his book.

What he really loved was attention, and trouble. In 1968, McLain found plenty of both, and found a way to put them together.

The Detroit newspapers were on strike for much of that summer, but that didn't stop Denny. On May 5, after a win over the California Angels that lifted his record to 4–0, McLain told the reporters who were there that Tiger fans were "the biggest front-running fans in the world.

"I don't care if I get booed here the rest of my life," McLain said. "Detroit is a great town. I like it. I've bought a home here and have roots. But the fans in this town are the worst in the league."

McLain tried to amend his comments, but never denied them.

"I tried to apologize in every way I could, but it was too late to get my foot out of my mouth," he wrote.

He would get the fans back on his side that season, because he kept winning. And fans everywhere love winners.

McLain was 14–2 by the end of June, 21–3 by the end of July. He would later write that his arm was hurting all the way, that he only got by with the help of ice, aspirin, and alcohol. He was in search of 30 wins, and he was in search of a $100,000 contract.

WINNINGEST SEASONS IN TIGERS HISTORY

31	**29**	**29**	**27**	**26**
DENNY MCLAIN	HAL NEWHOUSER	GEORGE MULLIN	DIZZY TROUT	HAL NEWHOUSER
1968	1944	1909	1944	1944

He got the 30 wins with three starts to spare. He'd settle for a little more than a 100 percent raise, from a $30,000 salary in 1968 to $65,000 in 1969.

He beat the Oakland A's on September 14 at Tiger Stadium for the landmark win, and had to come back out of the clubhouse because the fans kept chanting, "We want Denny! We want Denny!"

"I thought for a moment about all that had happened since I'd called them the 'worst fans anywhere' back in early May," McLain would write later. "People sure forgive a winner, don't they?"

McLain won the first of his two straight Cy Young Awards. The Tigers went on to win the World Series. But this is Denny McLain, so there was one more notable moment first.

It came in the eighth inning of his next start, with McLain well on the way to his 31st win. It was what was expected to be Mickey Mantle's final at-bat in Detroit, and McLain decided to groove one for him. He ended up having to groove three, because Mantle took the first two, but sure enough McLain gave up a home run, the 535th (and next-to-last) of Mantle's career.

"I cherish it as one of my warmest baseball memories," McLain would write.

Only Denny.

Bill Freehan's

11

All-Star Games

When the Tigers announced in 2011 that they were retiring No. 11 to honor Sparky Anderson, Denny McLain had one question:

Why not honor Bill Freehan, too?

Fair question. The Tigers have been traditionally stingy when it comes to retiring numbers. They've only retired six, and with the exception of Anderson and Willie Horton, they've only honored players who went into the Hall of Fame as Tigers. Anderson went into the Hall of Fame with a Reds cap, but he was also the winningest manager in Tiger history. Horton was not a Hall of Famer, but he was a hometown hero who also happened to be owner Mike Ilitch's favorite player (and has in recent years served as a club ambassador and special advisor).

So what about Freehan?

He never made the Hall of Fame, but he did make 11 All-Star teams. Only Al Kaline, with 18, was honored more times as a Tiger.

Freehan won five Gold Gloves, and twice finished in the top three in American League MVP voting.

"Freehan was the very best catcher we have had here in Detroit in the past 40-plus years," McLain wrote in an online column in 2011. "He knew the game better than anyone I ever played with or for. He was the on-field manager of our great Tiger teams, and he really knew more about situational baseball than anyone I ever met."

Freehan is an interesting case, because the honors during his playing career show that he had respect from players, fans, and the entire baseball community then. He was the All-Star starter seven times; the only AL catchers who started more All-Star Games were Ivan Rodriguez (12) and Yogi Berra (11).

And yet, when Freehan appeared on the Hall of Fame ballot in 1982, he got just two of the 415 votes, not even enough to remain on the ballot for a second year.

Whether or not he deserved more, Freehan absolutely deserves credit for what he did for the Tigers. The kid who was born in Royal Oak and grew up taking the bus to Tiger Stadium, the kid who once played against Horton in a Little League all-star game, became one of the most important players on a Tiger team that won a championship.

Freehan was a football and baseball star in high school, and his desire to play both sports in college led him to the University of Michigan (Notre Dame, his first choice, had insisted he choose between the two). As it turned out, Freehan played only one year

MOST GAMES CAUGHT, TIGERS

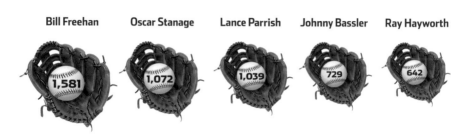

Bill Freehan	Oscar Stanage	Lance Parrish	Johnny Bassler	Ray Hayworth
1,581	1,072	1,039	729	642

of varsity football and varsity baseball before signing with the Tigers in 1961 for a $100,000 bonus. Freehan went on to get his degree from Michigan, in part because he made a deal with his father that he wouldn't get the bonus money until he graduated.

Freehan played in four big-league games in '61, and was back in the big leagues for good two years later. He made his first All-Star team in 1964, and was on the AL team for 10 years in a row. He was the All-Star starter seven straight years, from 1966 to 1972.

His offensive numbers don't look great by today's standards—a .262 career batting average, 15–20 home runs most years—but in the pitcher-dominated baseball of 1967–68, Freehan was the best hitting catcher in the game.

During his career, he was the AL All-Star starter 7 times.

Even so, it was his defense and his leadership that mattered more to the Tigers, and to Freehan himself.

"I wanted to hit well, of course," he would say. "I just never put that ahead of my primary responsibility. The catcher has to be the captain of the field. I felt if I did my job behind the plate, I was contributing to the team in the best way I could."

The pitchers trusted him. The Tigers trusted him.

"We put the full load on Freehan's shoulders," general manager Jim Campbell said. "And he didn't stumble."

Freehan played almost every game. He played 1,581 games behind the plate in his Tiger career, 509 more than any other catcher in franchise history. Five times, Freehan caught more than 130 games in a season.

He caught the All-Star Game, too, and in those days there was no such thing as a cameo appearance. When the 1967 game in Anaheim went 15 innings, Freehan caught all 15.

That year, Freehan finished third in MVP voting, behind Triple Crown–winner Carl Yastrzemski and Harmon Killebrew. The Tigers won 91 games, losing out to the Red Sox on the final day of the season.

"There is crying in baseball," said Jim Price, who was Freehan's backup on that team. "We cried that day. To play that hard and lose was tough."

Freehan took it as hard as anyone, knowing what a World Series would have meant to the city in that difficult summer of '67—and believing, as all the Tigers did, that they should have won.

"Shoot, we knew we were the best," he told George Cantor the following spring. "We thought we'd win easily. Maybe you have to learn that nothing comes to you. You have to take it."

The Tigers did take it in 1968. McLain, who won 31 games, was voted Most Valuable Player. This time, Freehan was second in the voting.

He was a star, an All-Star year after year. Maybe he wasn't a Hall of Famer, but he certainly was one of the best Tigers ever.

Eventually, the Tigers did retire his uniform number. But they didn't retire it for him.

Should they retire No. 11 again?

It's a fair question.

Norm Cash hits

.361

in 1961

No one has the career Norm Cash had.

Nobody has a season like Cash did at age 26, then plays another 13 years without coming close to repeating it.

Al Kaline won his only batting title at age 20, but he retired 20 years later as a .297 career hitter with 399 home runs. Cash won the batting title with a season worthy of the Hall of Fame, then spent the rest of his career as a player who was good but never great.

Cash's 1961 season stands up well under the so-called modern metrics, which credit him with a 201 OPS+. That means that even when equalizing for hitting in Tiger Stadium and in an expansion season where offense was up, Cash was twice as good as the average player.

Willie Mays never had a 201 OPS+. Albert Pujols never had a 201 OPS+. Hank Aaron never had a 201 OPS+.

You've heard of all the players who did: Babe Ruth, Ted Williams, Rogers Hornsby, Mickey Mantle, Lou Gehrig, Ty Cobb, Jimmie Foxx, Barry Bonds, Mark McGwire, Sammy Sosa, Frank Thomas, Jeff Bagwell, George Brett, Willie McCovey, Honus Wagner, Nap Lajoie—and Norm Cash.

That's 12 Hall of Famers, plus four guys who played in the steroid era—plus Norm Cash, a guy who got all of six votes in his lone year on the Hall of Fame ballot.

He wasn't a Hall of Famer. He did have one Hall of Fame year.

Cash later admitted that he had hollowed out the end of his bats in 1961, a common practice but one that was (and still is) against baseball rules. It hardly explains how he could have been so great that year, without ever approaching greatness again.

In his Tiger career, hit **373** home runs second to Kaline on the all-time franchise list.

But that was Norm Cash, a player who has been described both as one of the most popular players in Tiger history, and as one of the most-booed players. He could play hard but also laugh hard.

"There was no one else like him," teammate Gates Brown would say.

He hit 373 home runs in his Tiger career, second to Kaline on the all-time franchise list. He also struck out 1,081 times, third all-time behind Brandon Inge and Lou Whitaker.

He's the guy famous for carrying a table leg to home plate during Nolan Ryan's 1973 no-hitter, telling the umpire, "I can't hit him with a bat. I might as well try this."

He's also the only man who hit four home runs that cleared the Tiger Stadium roof.

NORM CASH'S 1961 SEASON

Batting average ▶ **.361***

Hits ▶ **193***

Home Runs ▶ **41**

RBIs ▶ **132**

On-base pct. ▶ **.487***

Slugging pct. ▶ **.662**

OPS ▶ **1.148***

OPS+ ▶ **201**

* Led League

Cash came to the Tigers from the Cleveland Indians in April 1960, in a steal of a trade for Steve Demeter. He stayed until 1974, when he was unceremoniously released in August.

"I'm pleased with my performance over the years in Detroit, but not with the publicity I received here," Cash told the *Detroit News* the day he was released. "For the job I did here, I thought I was a little underrated to say the least."

Cash became one of Kaline's closest friends, and along with Kaline and Rocky Colavito (acquired from the Indians in a much bigger trade five days later), Cash gave the Tigers a middle of the order

TOP OPS, SINGLE SEASON, TIGER HISTORY

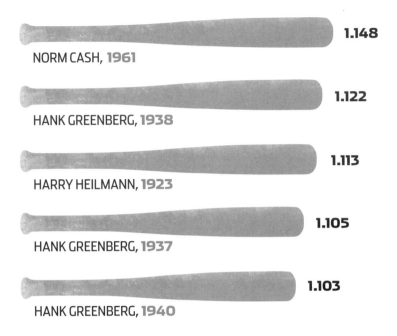

1.148

NORM CASH, 1961

1.122

HANK GREENBERG, 1938

1.113

HARRY HEILMANN, 1923

1.105

HANK GREENBERG, 1937

1.103

HANK GREENBERG, 1940

that was a match for the New York Yankees' trio of Roger Maris, Mickey Mantle, and Yogi Berra.

The '61 Yankees became one of baseball's legendary teams, a 109-win World Series champion, with Maris and Mantle both battling to top Babe Ruth's record of 60 home runs in a season (Maris finished with 61, Mantle with 54). The Tigers became one of the best runners-up baseball had ever seen. The '61 Tigers are one of just eight teams in history to win 100 games but miss out on the postseason.

Cash finished a distant fourth in MVP voting, behind not only the Yankee duo of Maris and Mantle, but also behind Baltimore's Jim Gentile. He did win the batting title, finishing 37 points ahead of his teammate Kaline, who was second.

He also had 41 home runs, 132 RBIs, and 124 walks.

Cash's on-base percentage of .487 is still a Tiger franchise record, while his slugging percentage of .662 ranks fourth in franchise history, behind Hank Greenberg's three best seasons. His unadjusted OPS of 1.148 is the best-ever by a Tiger.

It's also more than 200 points higher than Cash had in any of his other 16 big-league seasons.

"Norman used to say the dumbest thing he ever did was hit .361 that one season early in his career," teammate Jim Northrup told George Cantor years later. "Everyone was always waiting for him to hit like that again, and he just wasn't that kind of hitter. That was 1961, an expansion season. The pitching was down all over the league, and he had Kaline and Rocky Colavito, both having tremendous seasons, hitting around him.

"It wasn't going to happen like that for him again."

Fair enough, but no one else in baseball history has ever had a season quite like that without ever coming anywhere close to duplicating it.

No one else had a career quite like Norm Cash.

Willie Horton's

36

Home Runs in 1968

Willie Horton's appeal to Tiger fans was never based on his numbers.

He was the local kid who made good. He was the guy who walked out on the streets of Detroit, in uniform, to calm the city during the 1967 riots. He was the guy who made that throw to save the 1968 World Series.

In a book on unbelievable Tiger numbers, it's hard to find one of Horton's that fits. But it hardly fits to do a book on Tiger history and not include Willie Horton.

So here he is, with his modest-sounding 36 home runs in 1968.

And here's why that number belongs: Because in the pitching-dominated year of 1968, 36 home runs was a whole lot of home runs. It tied Horton with San Francisco's Willie McCovey for the second most in the majors, behind Washington's Frank Howard. Horton also finished that season second in the American League in total bases (278), second in slugging percentage (.543), and second in OPS (.895).

When it came time for the writers to vote on the American League's Most Valuable Player, Horton finished fourth, behind teammates Denny McLain and Bill Freehan, who were first and second, and Boston's Ken "Hawk" Harrelson, who was third. Only two teams since the '68 Tigers have had three of the top four in MVP voting (the 1974 Oakland A's, who went second, third, and fourth, and the 1976 Cincinnati Reds, who went first, second, and fourth).

Horton played 15 years with the Tigers and hit 262 home runs, fourth in franchise history behind Al Kaline, Norm Cash, and Hank Greenberg (although Miguel Cabrera figures to pass him in 2015). The Tigers traded

In his first season he finished 8th in MVP voting in 1965.

him away in 1977, and he wore five other uniforms in his final 3½ big-league seasons (and coached for two other teams).

In his heart, he never really left. When he could return, he did, and five decades on from winning a World Series, he's a familiar sight around town and around Comerica Park.

"If you cut out my heart and put it on a table, you'd see it has the Old English 'D' all over it," Horton once said.

The Tigers don't normally retire numbers for players who don't make the Hall of Fame. They made an exception for Horton, retiring his number in July 2000 and unveiling a statue that stands at Comerica Park.

And why not? If Kaline will always be Mr. Tiger, maybe Horton can be Mr. Detroit baseball.

He grew up in the city, not all that far from Tiger Stadium. He worked at the stadium as a junior usher, and played there in the city championship game for Northwestern High. And when it came time for him to sign a professional contract, in that era before the draft determined where a player would go, there was never a doubt that Willie Horton would be a Tiger.

He signed in August 1961, and debuted in the big leagues in September 1963. He was thrilled to meet his idol Rocky Colavito, and shocked that November when the Tigers traded Colavito in part because they knew Horton was on the way.

Horton's first full season was 1965, and he was so good so fast that he finished eighth in MVP voting that year.

The fans loved him, right from the start.

Author George Cantor, who covered generations of Tiger teams, maintained that Horton was the one player Tiger fans would never boo. They booed Kaline and Cash and McLain and Lolich, but never Willie.

His efforts during the riots have never been forgotten, and neither has that throw, the one that got Lou Brock at the plate in the fifth inning of Game 5. The Tigers trailed the World Series three games to one, and the Cardinals led the fifth game, 3–2. Brock was out, Kaline's two-run single in the seventh put the Tigers ahead, and the next two games went the Tigers' way.

"They say that [throw] turned the Series around," Horton would say.

Yes, they do say that, just as they say Willie Horton will always be one of the most popular players to wear a Tiger uniform.

They say it, and they're right.

And, come to think of it, Horton's 36 home runs in 1968 were kind of a big deal.

Al Kaline Wins a Batting Title at Age

20

Al Kaline played 22 years and had 3,007 hits. The record books credit him with 399 home runs, although he actually hit 401 (and lost two of them to rainouts before the games and stats became official). He played in 18 All-Star Games. He has spent 62 years with the same franchise, and he's not done yet.

But if there's one number that will always be linked with Kaline, it's 20. Twenty as in age 20, as in how young he was when he won the American League batting title.

As a 19-year-old Bryce Harper once said, "Who doesn't know that? Winning a batting title at 20? That's special."

It's so special that the silver bat from that year is one of the few awards Kaline kept for himself. It's so special that in all the years baseball has been played, Ty Cobb is the only other 20-year-old to win a batting crown.

Al Kaline being awarded the 1955 American League batting championship on August 6, 1956, by Earl Hilligan (left), of the American League office. On the other side of Kaline, holding the bat, is Charlie Gehringer, vice president of the Tigers and a former holder of the title. *(Photo courtesy AP Images)*

Kaline had Cobb beat by a single day. He was the youngest batting champion ever in 1955, and 60 years later, he still is.

For years, Kaline considered it something of a curse.

"The worst thing that ever happened to me in the big leagues was the start that I had," he told *Sports Illustrated's* Jack Olsen, in a story headlined "The Torments of Excellence." "Everybody said this guy's another Ty Cobb, another Joe DiMaggio. How much pressure can you take?"

This was in May 1964, when Kaline was struggling, the fans were booing and the Tigers were headed for yet another fourth-place finish. It wasn't enough then for him to just be Al Kaline, not when his early success had people thinking he was going to be the next coming of Cobb or Detroit's answer to Mickey Mantle.

It wasn't enough then. It's plenty enough now, and Bryce Harper isn't the only current player to look back and marvel at what Al Kaline did when he was just 20 years old.

Kaline had already played a full season in the big leagues. He'd come to the Tigers straight from his Baltimore high school, because of the "bonus baby" rule that required a big-league roster spot for anyone signing for $6,000 or more. He'd proven himself as an outfielder, but his offensive numbers as a 19-year-old (.276, with a .347 slugging percentage) were nothing special.

He was still a kid then. He came back in 1955 with a new uniform number (6), a new wife (Louise), a new contract (for $9,000), and enough added bulk that he was starting to look like a man.

Soon enough, he showed he could play like one.

AL KALINE'S TOP BATTING AVERAGES

1955 ▶ **.340**

1959 ▶ **.327**

1961 ▶ **.324**

1956 ▶ **.314**

1958 ▶ **.313**

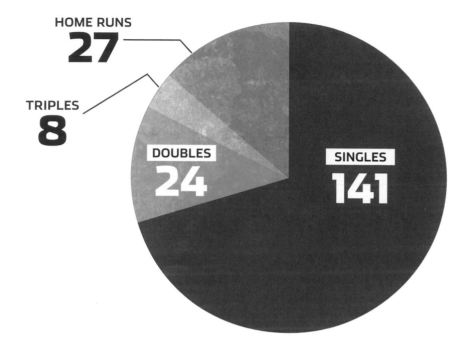

AL KALINE'S 200 HITS IN 1955

HOME RUNS
27

TRIPLES
8

DOUBLES
24

SINGLES
141

Kaline had two hits on Opening Day in Kansas City, and two more the next day, too. He had two triples in the Tigers' home opener, bringing new manager Bucky Harris to say, "I don't think the kid knows what pressure is."

The season went on, Kaline kept hitting, and the praise kept coming.

"He's the best 20-year-old I've ever seen," Harris would say.

Kaline said the two triples in the home opener gave him the feeling he belonged. He said he benefitted from pitchers challenging him early in the year, before they figured out he was a more mature and much improved hitter.

He had three home runs in a game later in the opening homestand ("Wake me up, somebody, I think I'm dreaming," he said as he sat in the dugout), and when he finally had his first 0-fer of the season on the final day of April, it only dropped his batting average to .429.

He had a four-hit game in May, and another one in June, and when the All-Star break came he was hitting .371. No one else in the majors was hitting better than .335. Kaline led the American League batting race by 45 points over Nellie Fox.

DiMaggio said Kaline "can't miss." Ted Williams said, "He's going to be one of the great right-handed hitters of baseball—if he isn't that already."

He got more All-Star votes than anyone but Yogi Berra and Roy Campanella, and not only did he start the game, he played the entire 12 innings and had a double and a walk.

By the end of July, Kaline led the AL in all three Triple Crown categories, but he was still telling people he wouldn't even lead his own team in hitting. Harvey Kuenn would beat him, Kaline said.

Kuenn scoffed at the idea.

... the youngest batting champion ever in 1955, and 60 years later, still is.

Kaline did have to survive a September slump (he was 3 for 34 at one point), but he won the title easily, finishing 21 points ahead of Vic Power.

"Everything I did was right that year," Kaline told biographer Jim Hawkins years later. "For a long time, the pitchers didn't think I was for real. By the time they found out, the season was over and I had the batting championship."

It was the only one he would ever win, but it was hardly the last time he would do something special.

No matter what Kaline did, he would always be the guy who won a batting title when he was 20. He would always remember it, too, and he has always championed other players getting a chance to play at a young age.

"If I could do it, more guys could," Kaline said, the spring the Washington Nationals were deciding on whether to keep the 19-year-old Harper in the big leagues.

Maybe more guys could do what Kaline did. The fact is that no one has.

Even Mike Trout, who nearly won the MVP award in 2012, turned 21 before that season ended. And Trout finished second to Miguel Cabrera in that year's batting race.

Some year, maybe there will be a batting champion younger than Kaline was in 1955. But don't count on it.

Baseball has been played for more than 100 years. And Al Kaline still stands alone.

Gates Brown's

106

Pinch Hits

Gates Brown showed up in the wrong era.

"He was ahead of his time," teammate Jim Price said years later. "He used a short bat, just like they use today."

He used a short bat, and he could really hit. As baseball people like to say, if you want to know what position the Gator played, the answer is simple: hitter.

"There are times you wonder if the guy can throw the ball across the street," manager Mayo Smith once said.

If Brown showed up today, he'd be a designated hitter, or they'd put him in the outfield every day and wouldn't worry much about his sub-par defense. He showed up in 1963, four years after the Tigers signed him out of the Ohio State Reformatory for $7,000, a full decade before the DH became part of baseball, and at a time when scores were low and defense was valued.

So Gates Brown became a sometimes outfielder and a most-of-the-time pinch hitter. He became a so-so outfielder who only once in 13 big-league seasons started even half his team's games in the field. He became a great pinch hitter who ended up with more career games coming off the bench than in the lineup.

You know how good a hitter you have to be for a team to keep you around year after year for one at-bat a night?

The Gator was that good.

"Gates was the only guy I can remember where the opposing manager managed the game with the idea of keeping him on the bench," Price said.

He had 106 career pinch hits, easily the most in Tiger history, and a third of them went for extra bases.

He had **106** career **pinch hits,** a third were for extra bases.

"A lot of people still think to this day...think Gates Brown is the best pinch-hitter of all time," Jim Leyland said in 2013.

Other pinch hitters had more career hits. Lenny Harris has the all-time record with 212, exactly twice as many as Brown had. But Brown's power and ability to take a walk gave him a career pinch-hit OPS of .779, far better than that of Harris or many of the others high on the all-time pinch hits list. It's even more impressive when you remember that most of Brown's pinch-hit appearances came during the 1960s, when pitchers dominated the game and batting averages were much lower.

His big hits and his big personality made him hugely popular in Detroit, where the biggest hits and the biggest stunts both became legendary. He was the guy who secretly ate hot dogs during games, the guy who once stuffed a hot dog inside his jersey when Smith called on him unexpectedly to pinch hit (he doubled to right and ended up with mustard on his jersey after a headfirst slide into second base).

GATES BROWN'S 106 CAREER PINCH HITS

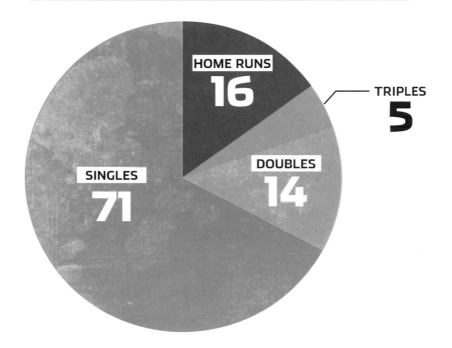

HOME RUNS
16

TRIPLES
5

DOUBLES
14

SINGLES
71

He was the high school football star who got in trouble and served 22 months for burglary. He was also one of the few people to earn a World Series ring in both 1968 and 1984, the first as a player, the second as hitting coach.

Brown played regularly as a 25-year-old outfielder in 1964, but that was his last year with 300 or more plate appearances until 1973, when the American League adopted the DH rule. Brown was the Tigers' first-ever DH, but he turned 34 that year and his skills were in decline.

It was nothing like 1968, when Brown had maybe the best season any pinch hitter has ever had. He reached base 26 of the 48 times Smith called on him to pinch hit (a .542 on-base percentage), and nine of his 18 hits went for extra bases.

And to think that the Tigers had tried to trade him away over the previous winter, and that Brown almost didn't make the team out of spring training.

Things changed quickly. The Tigers had lost on Opening Day, and Denny McLain couldn't hold a three-run lead in the season's second game. It was 3–3 in the ninth when Smith sent the Gator up to bat for the pitcher.

> **In a pinch, he reached base 26 of the 48 times, and nine of his 18 hits went for extra bases.**

The ball landed in the upper deck. The Tigers had their first win, and the Gator had his first big hit in his biggest season.

His first 10 appearances that season were all as a pinch hitter, and Brown delivered five hits and a walk. By the middle of June, he had only 22 at-bats, but already 11 hits.

It was that way all year. To some extent, it was like that for Brown's entire career.

The fans loved it, and they loved him.

The Gator himself always wanted more. He always figured he could have done more.

"That was never a dream, being a pinch hitter," he told author George Cantor years later. "Sitting on the bench for the whole game and then getting one swing. Who would want that? I wanted to play. Everyone who ever dreams of getting to the major leagues wants to be a star. No one sees themselves spending a career sitting on the bench."

If Brown had been born 10 years later, there's little doubt he would have spent much of his career as a DH. As it was, he had the misfortune to play just before the rules changed, and in an era (and for a manager) where poor defense could keep you on the bench.

It wasn't always that way. Rudy York had a reputation as a bad defender. Plenty of players did, but teams found spots for them because they could hit.

The Tigers found a spot for the Gator, but it was on the bench, waiting for his one chance a night.

"He's Tiger baseball," Dave Dombrowski said, on the day in 2013 when Brown passed away. "He's Tiger baseball for so many years. And he brought a smile to your face because of some of the stories you used to hear about him."

The stories, and the hits, they were all a part of the Gator's legacy. Maybe there would have been more of both if he'd played in a different era.

But maybe there wouldn't have been. Maybe it's best that Gates Brown is known as a pinch hitter—as the best pinch hitter the Tigers, or perhaps any team, ever had.

Earl Wilson's

7

Home Runs in 1968

The year Miguel Cabrera won the Triple Crown, he hit a home run once every 14.1 at-bats.

In 1968, Earl Wilson homered once every 12.6 at-bats.

In case you're not old enough to remember, yes, Earl Wilson was a pitcher. He was a pitcher who gave up a few home runs. And he was a pitcher who hit home runs.

It's probably not fair to call him the best power-hitting pitcher in baseball history (someone might mention Babe Ruth). But it is true that over the last half-century, no pitcher hit more home runs than Earl Wilson.

He hit 33 as a pitcher, and two more as a pinch hitter. He pinch-hit 28 times in his career, including six times (without a hit) in 1968.

Wilson wasn't a great hitter (he had a .195 career batting average), but he was a powerful hitter. He homered once every 21 at-bats in his career, a better ratio than Al Kaline or Willie Horton.

He homered seven times in 1966, the year the Tigers acquired him in a midseason trade with the Boston Red Sox. He homered seven times again in 1968, including on Opening Day.

Yes, Opening Day. The year the Tigers won the World Series, Earl Wilson was their Opening Day starter. He could hit, but he could also pitch.

He was a 22-game winner in 1967, a good enough pitcher that hitters sometimes accused him of throwing a spitball. Catcher Bill Freehan told the *Detroit Free Press* years later that it was actually an overthrown slider that would back up, but that he let hitters think it was a spitter.

In 1968, Earl Wilson homered once every 12.6 at-bats.

Wilson had a 2.85 ERA in 1968, one of the best of his career. However, in a year when Denny McLain won 31 games and Mickey Lolich won three games in the World Series, Wilson's pitching has been forgotten.

His hitting has not.

Tiger pitchers don't come to the plate these days, except in interleague games on the road. The idea of a pitcher hitting seven home runs in a season seems somewhat amazing.

But really, it was then, too.

In 1968, when Wilson hit seven home runs, no other pitcher hit more than three. No other Tiger pitcher hit even one.

Seventy-nine major league players (including Roger Maris) had at least 300 plate appearances that season without hitting seven home runs. Earl Wilson hit seven, in just 92 trips to the plate.

From the time Wilson joined the Tigers in 1966 until two weeks before he was traded away in 1970, no Tiger pitcher other than Earl Wilson hit a home run.

He hit 17.

"To me, it was another weapon I had as a pitcher," Wilson told author George Cantor. "It infuriated me when they brought in the designated hitter."

Wilson was done pitching (and hitting) by then. He had returned to Detroit, explaining to Cantor that he fell in love with the city

MOST HOME RUNS HIT, PITCHERS, 1951–2014

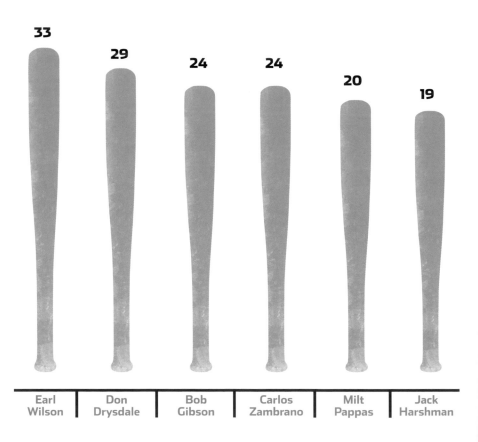

33	29	24	24	20	19
Earl Wilson	Don Drysdale	Bob Gibson	Carlos Zambrano	Milt Pappas	Jack Harshman

because it was the first place he had seen where there was a visible black middle class.

Wilson went into business, and also served as president of the Baseball Assistance Team, an organization devoted to helping former players who were down on their luck. He was successful in retirement, perhaps even more successful than he had been as a player.

In 1968 Wilson had a 2.85 ERA, one of the best of his career.

"Maybe I didn't achieve as much as I should have as a player," he told Cantor. "And maybe I achieved more than I should have in business. I'll take that tradeoff."

He is remembered, though. If nothing else, he's remembered as the pitcher who hit home runs.

There's nothing wrong with that.

Frank Lary's

28

Wins Over the Yankees

Between 1955 and 1961, the New York Yankees played in six World Series in seven years. The Yankees averaged 95 wins a year, and were 250 games over .500.

And they couldn't beat Frank Lary.

Lary faced the Yankees 45 times in those seven seasons, with a 27–10 record. No other pitcher beat them more than 16 times. No other pitcher with even 15 decisions had a record even two games over .500 against the Yankees.

Frank Lary never did anywhere near as well against any other opponent. In fact, for his career, Lary was a sub-.500 pitcher (100–103) against everyone but the best team in the game.

He really was "the Yankee Killer," even if his other numbers suggest he really didn't pitch that much different against the Yankees than he did against anyone else. His career ERA against the Yankees was 3.32. His career ERA in all other games was 3.52.

Lary was a good pitcher, but hardly a great one. He was twice a 20-game winner and once finished fourth in the American League ERA race, but no one would say he was one of the best pitchers of his era.

But in Detroit and even in New York, the "Yankee Killer" nickname stuck.

He earned it starting in 1956, when he went 5–1 against the Bombers. He had it for good by 1958, when he shut out the Yankees twice in a week, the first time on four hits and the second time on six.

A year later, Lary threw a 10-inning shutout against the Yankees at Briggs Stadium.

"I just throw them that breaking stuff of mine," Lary would say, when people asked about his success.

Others suggested that he changed speeds better than most pitchers, and kept the big hitters off balance. But it's not like he shut them down. Mickey Mantle had a .297 career average against Lary, with nine home runs. Roger Maris hit .330 against him, with eight homers.

It didn't matter. Lary won most of the games, and the result was that when the Tigers had a chance to set up their rotation, they

BEST CAREER WINNING PERCENTAGE VS. YANKEES, MINIMUM 20 WINS

.683   .677   .676   .652

Frank Lary   Dave McNally   Firpo Marberry   Jim Palmer

FRANK LARY VS. THE YANKEES

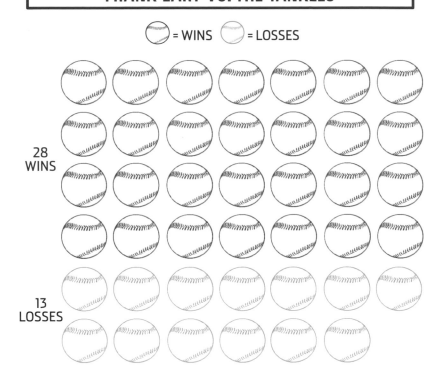

○ = WINS ○ = LOSSES

28
WINS

13
LOSSES

always wanted to make sure that Lary would face the Yankees. He started against them 49 times in his career, 11 more times than he started against any other opponent.

Not that it helped the Tigers in the standings. They finished behind the Yankees every one of those seasons, even in 1959, when the Yankees slumped to 79 wins but the Tigers finished under .500 at 76–78 (with the Chicago White Sox winning the pennant).

And in 1961, when Lary (23–9) and the Tigers (101–61) were great against everyone, the Yankees were even better, and the Tigers couldn't catch them. Lary beat the Yankees four times that season, but the game that stuck with him was a 7–2 loss on September 2. The Tigers trailed the Yankees by just 1½ games going into the weekend, but the Yankees swept the series and the Tigers never again got close. The Tigers gave Lary a 2–0 first-inning lead in the Saturday game, but Lary couldn't hold it and eventually allowed a tie-breaking home run to Maris (Maris' 52nd of the season).

Lary did beat the Yankees two weeks later in Detroit, but by that time, the race was no longer close. He beat them again in the Tigers' 1962 home opener, but that was a costly win.

It was freezing on that mid-April day at Tiger Stadium, with gametime temperature listed at 36 degrees, and with "flurries of snow, a drizzling rain, and an icy gale" in the newspaper reports. Lary pitched seven innings, leaving the game only when he pulled a muscle in his thigh while running out a triple in the bottom of the seventh.

Whether it was the effects of pitching in the cold or changes he made because of the leg injury, Lary wasn't the same after that. A workhorse to that point, he never again started more than 14 games in a season. He told reporters that his arm didn't hurt, but that he just couldn't throw as hard as he had before.

He would face the Yankees nine more times over the seasons to come, but would never again beat them.

The Tigers sold Lary to the New York Mets in May 1964. A year and a half later, he was out of baseball at age 35.

He had a nice career, and an even nicer distinction. At a time in baseball when the Yankees couldn't be beat, Frank Lary became known as "the Yankee Killer."

Magglio Ordonez Hits

.363

in 2007

Magglio Ordonez never did win a World Series.

He was a star with the White Sox, but left as a free agent eight months before they won their first championship in 88 years. He hit the home run that put the Tigers in the 2006 World Series, but he went 2 for 19 against the Cardinals and his teammates didn't do much better.

He retired before the Tigers got to the World Series again, and later was elected mayor of a city in Venezuela.

He's had a fine life, and he had a fine career. He'll always have that home run off Huston Street in 2006.

And he'll always have the 2007 season that ended with champagne—for drinking, not spraying.

"We're not champions this year," Jim Leyland said. "But out of respect for a teammate who accomplished something extraordinary, we all quietly poured a little glass of champagne."

Magglio deserved it.

He became the first Tiger in 46 years (since Norm Cash in 1961) to win a batting title. His .363 average was the highest by a Tiger in 70 years, since Charlie Gehringer hit .371 in 1937.

"To tell you the truth, I don't know how I did it, but I did it," Ordonez said. "I can't explain it. I just tried to get a hit every at-bat."

MAGGLIO ORDONEZ'S BEST TIGER BATTING AVERAGES

2007 ▸ **.363**

2008 ▸ **.317**

2009 ▸ **.310**

2010 ▸ **.303**

There were days in 2007 where it felt like he did just that. Ordonez had six four-hit games and 19 three-hit games. He hit safely in 124 of the 157 games he played.

He hit .421 in June, and .393 over the final two months of the season. He won the batting crown by 12 points over Ichiro Suzuki, he led the league in doubles (54), and he finished second in RBIs (139). He hit .429 with runners in scoring position, and an amazing .676 (25 for 37) with a runner on third and less than two out.

It was a remarkable season, the best season Ordonez ever had, one of the best a Tiger has had, at least since the days of Ty Cobb.

It was an interesting year for the Tigers, who won 88 games but weren't able to match their surprise 2006 World Series run. They had great individual accomplishments—Placido Polanco had 200 hits and became the first major league second baseman ever to complete a full errorless season, Curtis Granderson's 23 triples were the most by a major leaguer in 58 years—but they fell out of first place for good in mid-August and finished eight games behind the division-winning Indians.

By the season's final week, the individual honors were all that remained, and the biggest focus of all was on Ordonez. He led

Magglio Ordonez watches a two-run homer leave the park. *(Photo Courtesy AP Photo/ Chris Carlson)*

Ichiro by eight points at the All-Star break, and by six points entering September.

But Ichiro "slumped" to .347 in September, and Ordonez kept right on going. By the final day, Ordonez could have gone hitless and still won the crown.

He didn't go hitless. He went 3 for 4, finishing the season on a seven-game hitting streak in which he hit .577.

When it was over, he stood in the Tiger dugout at U.S. Cellular Field in Chicago, speaking on the phone to Venezuelan president Hugo Chavez. Ordonez was only the second player from Venezuela to win a batting title (Andres Galarraga won one in 1993 with the Rockies).

BEST TIGER BATTING AVERAGE, LAST 50 YEARS

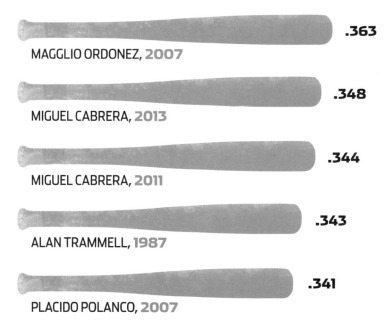

.363
MAGGLIO ORDONEZ, 2007

.348
MIGUEL CABRERA, 2013

.344
MIGUEL CABRERA, 2011

.343
ALAN TRAMMELL, 1987

.341
PLACIDO POLANCO, 2007

It was a special day for Venezuela, a special day for Ordonez, a special day for the Tigers.

"I want to thank the fans of Detroit," Ordonez said. "They deserve the batting title."

Magglio deserved it, too.

He had a better career than most people realize. He owns a higher

He hit safely in

124 of 157

games he played.

lifetime batting average (.309) than George Brett, Pete Rose, or Willie Mays. He had eight seasons where he hit .300, seven where he drove in 100 runs.

He won't be a Hall of Famer, but he's in that group of players who fall just a little short of deserving to be in.

He was part of turning the Tigers from losers into winners, signing as a free agent in February 2005. He stayed for seven years and hit .312. Over the last 50 years, only Miguel Cabrera has a better career average as a Tiger.

And no one, not even Cabrera, has had a season where he hit like Magglio Ordonez did in 2007.

Carlos Guillen's

3:30
AM Walk-Off Home Run

They headed home in the middle of the night, perhaps pleased that the freeways were empty, perhaps still amazed at what they had just seen. And perhaps thankful that when the sun came up in a couple of hours, it would be Saturday morning and the alarm clock might not be ringing.

There were plenty of them, Tiger fans who showed up for a game that was scheduled for 7:05 but didn't start until 11:06. Tiger fans who can tell you without lying that they stayed all the way to the end, all the way until they saw Carlos Guillen rounding the bases with the walk-off home run that beat the New York Yankees.

All the way until 3:30 AM.

The Tigers have never played another game like it.

"The first time I've ever hit a home run at 3:30 AM," Guilllen said.

Has anyone?

Other major league games have ended later in the night. There was a famous Phillies-Padres doubleheader in 1993 that ended at 4:40 AM. But that ended with a Mitch Williams single, and the last home run came five innings and probably an hour and a half earlier.

There was a famous 19-inning game in 1985 between the Braves and Mets that ended at 3:55 AM. Rick Camp homered in the 18th to tie that one. His homer could have been later in the night than Guillen's, but it wasn't a walk-off.

Newspaper reports at the time say there were about 8,000 still in the stands when the Braves-Mets game ended, mostly because the Braves promised to still shoot off their July 4 fireworks. About 10,000 stayed to the end at Comerica, with the promise of a win over the Yankees.

> **There was a famous Phillies-Padres doubleheader in 1993 that ended at 4:40 AM.**

"Hey, the bars were closed, man," Tiger pitcher Nate Robertson explained later that day. "Why would anyone go anywhere?"

Owner Mike Ilitch admitted that he had left early.

"The old-timer conked out," he said.

Those who stayed will never forget it. They saw a game started by 45-year-old Roger Clemens and 22-year-old Andrew Miller (who had once won the Roger Clemens Award). They saw Curtis Granderson's 20th and 21st triples, the most any major leaguer has had in a season since 1949. They saw a home run by Alex Rodriguez, who would win the MVP that year, and also by Magglio Ordonez, who would finish second.

And they saw a home run at 3:30 AM.

Why did it happen? Why did a game start after 11:00 PM?

Well, it was the Yankees' only trip to Detroit. The Saturday game was scheduled for 4:00 PM, making a day-night doubleheader

MOST WALK-OFF HOME RUNS, COMERICA PARK

In their 15 seasons at Comerica Park, the Tigers have ended 40 games with a walk-off home run. There's no doubt which is the most famous. It's the one Magglio Ordonez hit to send the Tigers to the 2006 World Series. But who has the most?

6 Brandon Inge

5 Miguel Cabrera

4 Carlos Guillen

2 Jhonny Peralta

2 Johnny Damon

2 Ivan Rodriguez

2 Shane Halter

impossible. Also, after a rainout in Chicago the night before, Major League Baseball had sent word to all umpiring crews to make every effort to avoid any more rainouts.

Some players weren't happy with the wait. Yankees manager Joe Torre wasn't happy.

But others chose to enjoy it.

"We're a 3:00 AM team," Tigers pitcher Kenny Rogers joked. "Back up the start times. The fans wouldn't mind. Did you see how many were still there?"

Tiger fans had some experience with long games against the Yankees. The longest game in Comerica Park history was a June 1, 2003, game against the Yankees, on a day Clemens was going for his 300th career win. A Tiger team headed for 119 losses rallied from a 7–1 deficit against a Yankee team headed for the World Series, before finally losing in 17 innings and 5 hours, 10 minutes.

The longest game in Tiger Stadium history was also a loss to the Yankees, on June 24, 1962. They played 22 innings and exactly 7 hours that day, before Jack Reed won it for the Yankees with a home run off Phil Regan.

But those games didn't feature walk-offs, and those games both began in the afternoon, not late at night.

Those games didn't end with Carlos Guillen circling the bases at 3:30 in the morning.

Only one game the Tigers have ever played ended like that. And if you were on those freeways headed home that night (or should we say early morning?), you won't soon forget it.

Carlos Pena's

6

Hit Game

The day the Tigers traded for Carlos Pena, I surveyed a handful of scouts to see what they thought.

Half thought he'd be a star. Half were equally sure he'd be a bust.

Turned out all of them were wrong.

Pena has played 14 seasons in the major leagues. He played in a World Series. He won a Silver Slugger. He won a Gold Glove. He even made an All-Star team. He's hardly been a bust.

He's also been released five times, and allowed to walk away quietly as a free agent countless others. He's hardly been a star.

But every now and then he would look like one.

May 27, 2004, was every now and then.

Pena was in an awful slump. He was 5 for 49 over the past three weeks. He was hitting .204 for the season, his second full season with the Tigers.

Then, on that May night in Kansas City, he had six hits in one game.

This was no normal game. For one thing, the Tigers had 27 hits, tying a nine-inning club record that had stood for 76 years. For another, they needed help from the Elias Sports Bureau to declare it a record, because for years, their records showed they had 28 hits in the September 29, 1928, game against the Yankees.

It turned out that Pinky Hargrave had long been credited with one too many hits (four, when he really had three) that day at Navin Field. So 27 was the record, and the 27 hits the Tigers had that night at Kauffman Stadium tied the record.

"It's not much fun being me," said Royals starter Brian Anderson, who gave up the first 12 hits.

For that one night, it was fun being a 2004 Tiger. It was especially fun being Carlos Pena.

He singled and scored in the second inning. He singled to drive in a run in the third. He doubled in the fifth. He singled in the sixth. He homered in the eighth. He homered again in the ninth.

That's 6 for 6, with 13 total bases, four runs scored, and five RBIs.

Other players have had days like that. Ty Cobb once had 16 total bases in a game. Dmitri Young had 15 the year before. Damion Easley had a six-hit game in 2001.

What made it such a Carlos Pena-like day was that he had been so bad for the three weeks before.

"This has been difficult for me, but what's past is past," he said that night. "Does the sand flow up in an hourglass? No, it doesn't. It's gone. The errors of yesterday can't be made right today."

Got that? Remember, this is the same guy who once explained a long slump by declaring, "Where the dry desert ends, the green grass grows."

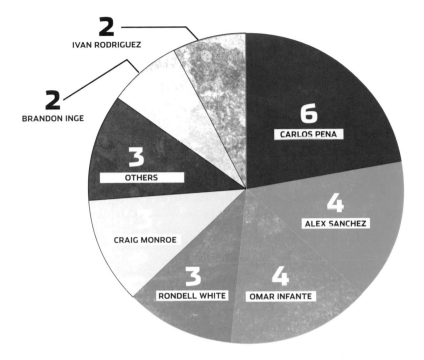

THE TIGERS' 27 HITS ON MAY 27, 2004

2 IVAN RODRIGUEZ

2 BRANDON INGE

6 CARLOS PENA

3 OTHERS

4 ALEX SANCHEZ

3 CRAIG MONROE

3 RONDELL WHITE

4 OMAR INFANTE

For Carlos Pena, a six-hit day didn't make the grass grow, and didn't put the hourglass right. Over the next week, he went 1 for 20 with six strikeouts.

In 3½ seasons as a Tiger, he was a .244 hitter (a little better than his career average) with a .792 OPS (a little worse). He was just 27 years old when the Tigers released him in the final days of spring training 2006.

"He's always been a very highly touted individual, a guy that still has a lot of ability," general manager Dave Dombrowski said that day. "It really comes down at some point to you have to put it together on the field."

From there, Pena was signed and released by the Yankees, signed and allowed to become a free agent by the Red Sox, and signed by the Devil Rays (where he played in the 2008 World Series after the team was renamed the Rays). He was signed and allowed to become a free agent by the Cubs, signed again by the Rays and again allowed to leave, signed and released by the Astros, signed by the Royals and allowed to leave, signed and released by the Angels, and signed and released by the Rangers.

It wasn't the career the Rangers had in mind when they drafted Pena with the 10th pick in the first round in 1998. It wasn't the career the A's had in mind when they traded for Pena four years later.

It certainly wasn't the career Dombrowski had in mind when he acquired Pena in his first big trade after becoming the Tigers GM.

There was more to that deal than Pena. Dombrowski really wanted to be rid of Jeff Weaver (another first-round pick who never lived up to the early billing). He got Jeremy Bonderman, who was a player to be named later on the day of the trade but ended up having as much success as anyone in the deal.

Bonderman eventually helped the Tigers to the World Series. Pena did not.

But every now and then, Carlos Pena really would look like a star.

May 27, 2004, was every now and then.

MOST HITS IN A GAME, TIGERS

27
MAY 27, 2004 at Royals

27
SEPTEMBER 29, 1928 vs. Yankees

26
SEPTEMBER 6, 2013 vs. Royals

26
JULY 5, 1936 at Browns

Craig Monroe Hits

5

October HRs (and So Does Delmon Young)

You always have to be careful talking about postseason records.

Brandon Inge played in 23 postseason games for the Tigers. So did Hank Greenberg.

Jhonny Peralta has more postseason home runs than Greenberg.

So what?

Inge and Peralta's postseason history includes the Division Series, the ALCS, and the World Series. Greenberg's postseason history is his World Series history.

But baseball's three-tiered October playoff has been around for two decades now, long enough to know that it's a big deal when someone hits five home runs in a single postseason. David Ortiz, for all his October heroics, has never homered more than five times in a single postseason.

Five October home runs isn't a major league record—Barry Bonds (2002 Giants), Nelson Cruz (2011 Rangers), and Carlos Beltran (2004 Astros) each hit eight—but five October home runs is a lot.

Especially for a guy who never hit 30 home runs in a full season. Or for two guys who never hit 30 in a season.

Magglio Ordonez hit the home run everyone remembers in October 2006, maybe the biggest home run in Tiger history, the

MOST HOME RUNS BY A TIGER, ONE POSTSEASON

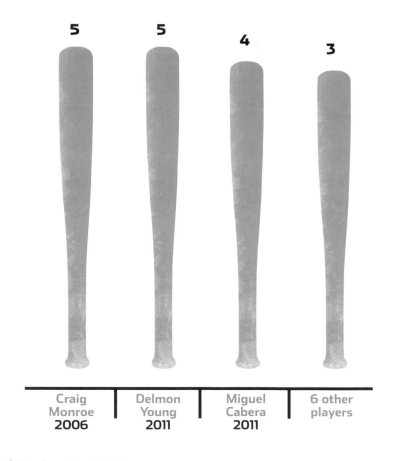

Craig Monroe 2006	Delmon Young 2011	Miguel Cabera 2011	6 other players
5	5	4	3

one that put the Tigers into the World Series. But Craig Monroe outhomered him that month, 5–3.

Justin Verlander was the Tigers' big star in 2011, winning the Cy Young and the MVP. But it was Delmon Young who nearly homered the Tigers into the World Series.

His seventh-inning home run in Game 3 against the New York Yankees gave the Tigers a 5–4 win and a two games to one edge in the Division Series. His first-inning homer gave the Tigers a crucial run in their 3–2 win in the decisive Game 5. And with the Tigers down three games to one in the ALCS against the Texas Rangers, it was Young's two home runs that won Game 5 and kept the series alive.

... a guy who never hit 30 home runs in a full season.

The Tigers didn't get to the World Series that year, but Young matched Monroe's club record with five October home runs. And he did it despite being left off the Tigers' original ALCS roster, because of a strained oblique. The Tigers added Young back to the roster before Game 2 against the Rangers only because Ordonez got hurt.

He was an unlikely October hero. Then again, Monroe had been one, too.

Monroe came to the Tigers in February 2002, on a waiver claim from the Rangers. Then he spent that season getting called up and sent back down. Monroe started the season at Triple-A Toledo. He played two games with the Tigers in late April, one game in May, then back to Toledo. Two games in June, then back to Toledo. One game in July and…you guessed it, back to Toledo.

Dick Egan, the scout who recommended Monroe to the Tigers, would tell friends that he got banned from even asking about Monroe, because he called so many times telling the front office to give Monroe a chance.

The chance came in 2003, and Monroe was part of the team that lost 119 (but not 120) games. He was one of the 12 players from the 2003 team who was also an American League champion with the 2006 Tigers.

Monroe was done as a Tiger a year later, designated for assignment to make room on the roster for Cameron Maybin, then traded to the Chicago Cubs for Clay Rapada. It was a quiet finish for a player who had a mostly quiet Tiger career, but was front and center for one very important month.

Young's Tiger career was even briefer and less distinguished. Really, except for those five October home runs, he's better known for being Dmitri Young's kid brother, or for being the guy suspended after being accused of using anti-Semitic language in a street altercation in New York.

The Tigers acquired Young in an August 2011 trade with the Minnesota Twins. They allowed him to leave as a free agent after 2012.

In between, Delmon Young had one big month at a very big time. He hit five postseason home runs in 2011, just as Craig Monroe did in 2006.

Ivan Rodriguez Signs

$40

Million Contract

It's hard to describe how stunning it was to see Ivan Rodriguez sign with the Tigers.

He was just coming off winning a World Series. They were just coming off losing 119 games.

He had been to the playoffs four times in the last eight seasons. They hadn't made the playoffs in 17 years.

He went to the All-Star Game 10 straight years. They were going on nine straight years without having more than the minimum one lone All-Star.

He already looked like a surefire Hall of Famer. They'd gone 30 years (since Al Kaline retired) without having any player who had Cooperstown in his future.

It was understandable that the Tigers wanted to start turning things around, after enduring the most embarrassing season in their long history. It was unbelievable that they'd be able to start turning it around with Pudge Rodriguez.

"I know they had a bad season last year," Rodriguez said at his introductory press conference. "But I think this is going to be a completely different season.... You're going to see this organization, this Detroit Tigers team, in the playoffs soon."

It sounded crazy. It turned out to be true.

It also turned out to be one of the most significant signings in Tiger history. Pudge had some issues during his time in Detroit— his relationship with manager Alan Trammell and bench coach Kirk Gibson was hardly smooth—but his presence gave the Tigers a sense of credibility that they wouldn't lose for the next decade-plus.

Won 3 more Gold Gloves, giving him 13, most ever for a catcher.

The Tigers had already signed Fernando Vina, Rondell White, and Jason Johnson in that winter of 2003–04, as they tried to recover from the losingest season an American League team had ever had. Vina, White, and Johnson were better than the overmatched players the Tigers already had, but none was close to being the kind of player who could turn a franchise around.

Pudge Rodriguez was.

He shouldn't have been available to them. Rodriguez had played for $10 million in his one championship year with the Marlins, and the word was that he was looking for a four-year deal for the same annual salary. It didn't seem unreasonable, but Rodriguez was also coming off three consecutive seasons in which he had missed time with injuries. He had just turned 32.

Agent Scott Boras needed a team that would take the chance, and Tigers owner Mike Ilitch needed a signing that would prove to people that he cared about his baseball team as much as he did

Pudge Rodriguez adjusts his new cap during the press conference announcing his four-year, $40 million contract with the Tigers. *(Bill Pugliano)*

about his hockey team. Rodriguez and Ilitch hit it off, and Ilitch's front office structured a contract that gave Pudge his $40 million for four years, but also offered the Tigers some protection against injury.

"This is how it starts," Trammell said. "This is how we get better."

It turned out to be a great deal, although not so great for Trammell.

Rodriguez made the All-Star team in all four seasons. He won three more Gold Gloves, giving him 13, the most ever for a catcher. He

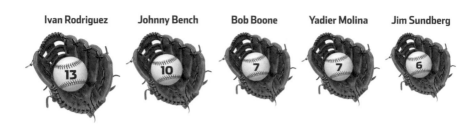

Ivan Rodriguez	Johnny Bench	Bob Boone	Yadier Molina	Jim Sundberg
13	10	7	7	6

batted .334 in 2004, the highest average by a Tiger since Trammell in 1987. For a while that summer, it looked like he might become the first catcher ever to win a batting title.

Oh, and that prediction he made about the Tigers going to the playoffs "soon"? They were in the World Series before Pudge's contract was up.

Signing Pudge didn't get them there, not by itself. The Tigers signed Magglio Ordonez the next winter, and Kenny Rogers the winter after that. They used the high draft pick generated by their awful 2003 finish to draft Justin Verlander, then brought him to the big leagues as a 23-year-old Rookie of the Year.

But when the 2006 World Series began, it was Pudge Rodriguez who was behind the plate.

It was stunning to see the Tigers in the World Series that year, just three years removed from losing 119 games. But no more stunning than it was to see them sign Pudge Rodriguez, just a few months after that 119th loss.

Armando Galarraga's

28

Out Perfect Game

According to all available records, no Tiger pitcher has ever thrown a perfect game. But everyone who was at Comerica Park on June 2, 2010, knows it happened. Everyone who was paying attention to baseball that night or in the days to follow knows it happened.

Armando Galarraga threw a perfect game.

We saw it. We know it. And it doesn't really matter if the official baseball records say he didn't.

He threw a perfect game. In fact, it was better than perfect, because most pitchers only need to get 27 outs without allowing a batter to reach first base.

Galarraga got 28. Twenty-eight Cleveland Indians came to the plate, and 28 Cleveland Indians made outs.

It was perfect—a 28-out perfect game.

That's how I remember it.

You're welcome to think of it as the Jim Joyce game, because it was Joyce's blown call on the 27th out that forced Galarraga to get that 28th out. I prefer to think of it as a 28-out perfect game, because on that night, Armando Galarraga had to be better than perfect—and he was.

There's never been another game like it. With video replay now in use, it's pretty safe to say there will never be another game like it ever again.

28 Cleveland Indians came to the plate, and 28 Cleveland Indians made outs.

As special as a perfect game is—there have only been 23 of them in major league history—what Galarraga did that night is even more unlikely, even more special.

He retired the first 26 Indians he faced that night. He retired the 27th—Jason Donald—as well, but first-base umpire Jim Joyce blew the call. The Tigers argued, and they were right, but there was no replay review to fix the mistaken call.

So Galarraga went back to the mound, threw five more pitches, and got Trevor Crowe to ground to third for an out, the 28th out of his never-to-be-duplicated perfect game.

Joyce went to the umpires room, saw the replay, and apologized while in tears. Galarraga went to the Tiger clubhouse, accepted his teammates' congratulations, and refused to share their anger. Joyce asked to see Galarraga, the two hugged, and the pitcher told the umpire, "It's all right. Mr. Joyce, this stuff it just happens."

It's all right?

For the rest of us it sure wasn't, not at first and maybe not even later. We didn't understand how Armando Galarraga, a 28-year-old Venezuelan who began the season in Triple-A, could throw what should have been a perfect game. We really didn't understand how Jim Joyce, a well-respected veteran umpire, could blow it for him.

Armando Galarraga with the ball as Jason Donald reaches the bag for what should have been the 27th and final out of a perfect game. Umpire Jim Joyce, however, disagreed. *(Bill Eisner/Detroit Tigers)*

It wasn't like it was a tough call. Replay would have overturned it, but this wasn't one that required slow motion or stop-action. Everyone saw it—clearly—except that in the moment he had to make the call, Jim Joyce somehow saw it clearly the other way.

A few hours earlier, Ken Griffey Jr. announced his retirement in Seattle. It was baseball's biggest story, all anyone was talking

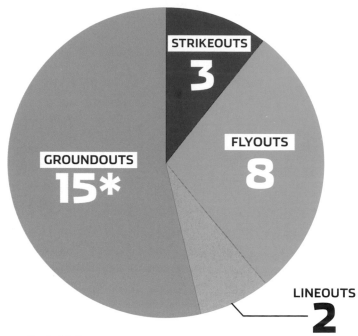

ARMANDO GALARRAGA'S 28 OUTS

STRIKEOUTS
3

FLYOUTS
8

GROUNDOUTS
15*

LINEOUTS
2

*One called a hit because
of umpire error

about, until a pitcher and an umpire in Detroit made history and made us think.

Fans credited Joyce with admitting his mistake. Galarraga won praise for taking it so well.

"People love the story," he said, when I asked him about it a few weeks later.

Michigan governor Jennifer Granholm issued a proclamation declaring that Galarraga had thrown a perfect game. Rep. John Dingell called on baseball to overturn Joyce's call, and writers and fans around the country rushed to agree with him.

GM North America presented Galarraga with a red Corvette convertible.

When the season ended, the pitcher and the umpire collaborated on a book.

Joyce continued to umpire, better known than ever. Galarraga continued to pitch, although the Tigers traded him to Arizona at the end of that 2010 season, and he moved from team to team and spent much of the next two years in the minor leagues.

In his next 12 starts after the 28-out perfect game, Galarraga never carried a perfect game through the second inning, let alone through the seventh or eighth. He started another 34 major league games (and another 39 minor-league games), without a single complete-game win.

He faded from view, to the point where his name only brings a hint of recognition for most fans.

Yeah, he's the guy, the guy who had a perfect game taken away from him.

He's the guy, the guy who once threw a 28-out perfect game, the only one there ever was, the only one there ever will be.

Virgil Trucks Throws

2

No-Hitters in One Season

It's pretty safe to say there's never been a season like the one Virgil Trucks had for the 1952 Tigers.

He lost 19 games, and won only five. He had two games where he gave up 13 hits.

And also two games where he gave up none.

He no-hit the Washington Senators in May, in a game he started with an 8.47 ERA. He no-hit the New York Yankees in August, shutting down the best hitting team in the American League (and the team that would go on to win the World Series).

Trucks also one-hit the Senators in July, which means that three of his five wins came in games where he gave up one hit or none.

And it's not just wins. Take out those three games (of the 35 he pitched in that year), and Trucks' ERA of 4.61 would have ranked fourth-worst in the majors.

Modern metrics don't treat his season much better, assigning him an ERA-plus of 95 and a WAR of 1.8 (which ranked tied for 52nd among big-league pitchers).

He didn't have a good year, and neither did the Tigers, who had the first 100-loss season in franchise history.

The Tigers didn't have a good off-season, either, trading Trucks to the St. Louis Browns in a six-player deal that brought them back nothing of real value.

"I thought [the trade] was awful," Trucks would later say, even though he went on to win 20 games in 1953 (five for the Browns, 15 after he was traded to the Chicago White Sox in June). "I would have loved to stay with Detroit my whole career."

> *Modern metrics don't treat his season much better, assigning him an ERA-plus of 95 and a WAR of 1.8.*

The Tigers actually made a trade to reacquire Trucks in November 1955, only to deal him away for a second time after the 1956 season.

If that sounds complicated, it's nothing compared to the stories about how the Tigers acquired Trucks in the first place. Reports at the time suggested they bought his contract for just $100. Tigers scout Eddie Goosetree, the story went, signed Trucks for that price as an outfielder.

But Trucks told author Burge Carmon Smith that the deal was more involved, and that by the time he actually went to the Tigers (as a pitcher), they had to pay $10,000 to his minor-league team in Andalusia, Alabama.

Whatever it was, it worked out for the Tigers. Trucks won 114 games for Detroit, plus one in the 1945 World Series. In fact, because he didn't come back from the Navy until late in the season, Trucks holds the distinction of winning a game in the World Series after not winning any in the regular season.

Trucks had a 16-win season before going off to the war, so he was already considered a big-time pitcher. When the Tigers clinched the 1945 pennant, Hank Greenberg told reporters the Tigers would win the Series because "[Hal] Newhouser will win two, and Trucks will win two."

Steve O'Neill, the Tigers manager, heaped even more praise on Trucks: "I think he is faster than [Bob] Feller and has the best curveball I've seen all year. He can't miss."

But Trucks hurt his arm in 1950. He became a different pitcher after that, relying more on curves and sliders than on a fastball that was supposedly once clocked at 105 mph (although the technology would have been so primitive that it's hardly worth using to compare him to pitchers today).

They were 6–18 when Trucks faced the Senators on May 15, one reason the game drew only 2,215 fans.

The Tigers got off to a horrible start in 1952, losing their first eight games and 17 of their first 21. They were 6–18 when Trucks faced the Senators on May 15, one reason the game drew only 2,215 fans. It probably didn't help that the city scheduled a parade that same day to honor General Douglas MacArthur.

Trucks had more problems. His feet were swollen, and he couldn't fit into his shoes. Teammate Art Houtteman offered his.

The other issue was that while Trucks wasn't allowing the Senators any hits, Washington starter Bob Porterfield wasn't allowing the Tigers any runs. When Trucks got through the top of the ninth with his no-hitter intact, he still couldn't celebrate because the game was still scoreless.

Fortunately for Trucks and the Tigers, Vic Wertz was due up in the ninth. Wertz, who already had the only extra-base hit of the day (a seventh-inning double), smashed a home run that gave the

Tigers the win and gave Trucks his no-hitter. It also gave Trucks a headache, because when he jumped off the bench to celebrate, he banged his head on the dugout roof.

The second no-hitter, on August 25 at Yankee Stadium, was seen by quite a few more fans (13,442). But it also had some suspense, with official scorer John Drebinger of the *New York Times* twice changing his call on a third-inning Phil Rizzuto ground ball.

Drebinger first gave Tiger shortstop Johnny Pesky an error on the play, then changed it to a hit. Then, after other writers complained, Drebinger called the Tiger dugout in the seventh inning to speak to Pesky himself. Pesky told Drebinger that he hadn't been able to get a grip on the ball, and that it should have been scored an error.

So it was, and by that point Trucks had just six outs to go. There were no more scares—and the Tigers had scored a run in the seventh—so the man they called "Fire" Trucks got his second no-hitter.

At the time, only Johnny Vander Meer and Allie Reynolds had thrown two no-hitters in one season. Later, Nolan Ryan would join them, and so would Roy Halladay (with one of Halladay's coming in the postseason).

None of them ever had a year like Trucks, a year that could be so bad and so good, all at the same time.

Les Mueller's

$19^2/_3$

Inning No-Decision

In the 20th inning of a game that would go 24, Tiger manager Steve O'Neill walked to the mound to rescue Les Mueller.

There were two out in the 20th, and Mueller had just walked his second Philadelphia Athletics batter of the inning. You could hardly blame him. That was the 74th batter Mueller had faced on that Saturday afternoon at Shibe Park.

We can only imagine how many pitches Mueller threw. We can only imagine how his arm must have felt. We do know that he had already thrown $19^2/_3$ innings.

We know it was the longest any pitcher had stayed in a game since 1929. We know—no surprise here—that Mueller is still the only man since 1929 to throw 19 innings in one game.

We also know that he didn't want to come out.

"You've had enough," O'Neill told him.

Mueller wanted more.

"It never occurred to me to come out of that game," Mueller said years later. "I felt okay."

The Tigers had just come from Washington, where they had played two doubleheaders in three days. O'Neill was determined to get innings out of Mueller, his Saturday starter.

Besides, in all those innings, Mueller had allowed just one unearned run on 13 hits. Future Tiger (and future Hall of Famer) George Kell was 0 for 8, on the way to an 0 for 10 day.

"[Hal] Newhouser told me I was still throwing as hard in the 20th inning as I had in the whole game," Mueller said.

O'Neill decided that 74 batters were enough. He called on Dizzy Trout, even though Trout had pitched 4⅔ innings the day before in Washington.

Trout got Dick Siebert to ground out to end the 20th and then pitched four more shutout innings.

It had been 1–1 since the seventh, when the Tigers' Roy Cullenbine scored on a Doc Cramer ground ball. The two teams combined to have 30 more baserunners (16 for the A's, 14 for the Tigers), but not one of them scored. The A's had a runner thrown out at the plate in the 10th. The Tigers hit into a double play with the bases loaded in the 24th.

It ended 1–1, called because of darkness, even though Shibe Park had lights. Lights were still new in baseball, and the rules said that if a game began without them, they couldn't be turned on midgame. So it ended as a tie, to be replayed as part of a doubleheader the next time the Tigers were in town.

The A's won the makeup game 3–2...in 16 innings.

The Tigers still won the pennant, by 1½ games over Washington. They won the World Series in seven games over the Chicago Cubs.

Mueller ended the season with a 6–8 record and 3.68 ERA. He pitched two scoreless innings in the World Series, the last two he'd ever pitch in the major leagues. He made it all the way through spring training with the Tigers in 1946, but was sent to Triple-A Buffalo just minutes before gametime on Opening Day.

Mueller spent the next three seasons in Triple-A, then retired at age 30.

> **Mueller ended the season with a 6–8 record and 3.68 ERA.**

"It just about broke my heart that Detroit didn't keep me in 1946," he said years later.

Mueller went home to Belleville, Illinois. In 1995, on the 50th anniversary of the 24-inning game, the Cardinals invited him to throw out the first pitch before a game in St. Louis.

He told reporters that day that he figures he threw about 370 pitches in his 19²/₃ innings. He also told them that he felt fine.

"I always kept hoping we'd get a run and I'd get a win, but it didn't work out that way," Mueller said.

The Tigers haven't played a 24-inning game since then. Their longest was a 22-inning game in 1962 against the Yankees, a game they lost 9–7. No pitcher in that game went more than eight innings, but the Yankees' Yogi Berra caught all 22 innings.

In the 24-inning game in 1945, both catchers went the distance— Bob Swift for the Tigers and Buddy Rosar for the A's.

"It was a pretty warm day in Philadelphia," Mueller said. "I think it would have been as hard or harder on him than it was on me."

George Kell Hits

.343

to Beat Ted Williams

The Tigers have had 11 players win batting titles, from the 12 that Ty Cobb won in the early years of the franchise to Miguel Cabrera's three straight in recent times. Two of the batting titles locked up the Triple Crown, by Cobb in 1909 and by Cabrera 103 years later.

Cobb and Al Kaline won a batting crown at age 20, the only two players in the history of baseball who were that young when they won. Norm Cash won in his first season as a full-time regular, and spent the rest of his career listening to people ask why he couldn't do it again.

Harry Heilmann won in 1921, even though the unofficial averages at the end of the season had him second to Cobb, his teammate and manager. Dale Alexander won in 1932, even though the Tigers traded him to the Boston Red Sox that June.

It's quite a list, one that also includes Heinie Manush, Charlie Gehringer, and Magglio Ordonez.

And George Kell, whose 1949 title may well have been the most special of all. He won it by beating out the man many still consider to be the best hitter who ever lived.

He won it by beating Ted Williams, on the final day of the season. He won it by costing Ted Williams the Triple Crown.

"You beat me fair and square, the way you're supposed to," Williams would tell Kell years later, after both men had been inducted into the Hall of Fame. "It was a great race. I loved it."

It was a great race, especially for Kell.

He was hitting .348 at the end of April, .353 at the end of June. But as he wrote in his book, *Hello Everybody, I'm George Kell,* he never thought he'd win the crown.

"I always thought [Williams] was right on the edge of piling up 10 hits in his next 15 at-bats to make a joke out of the batting race," Kell wrote.

Williams did go 9 for 18 in one five-day stretch in July, and 12 for 18 in one five-game stretch in August, so through August 11, he led Kell, .354 to .341. Williams still led by 12 points as the race headed into September, and by 10 points with just a couple of weeks to go.

> **He was hitting .348 at the end of April, .353 at the end of June.**

Then Kell got hot, and Williams got uncharacteristically cold. Entering the final day of the season, Williams' edge was down to three points, at .344 to .341. The Tigers were facing Cleveland's Bob Lemon, a 22-game winner who held opponents to a .210 batting average that season. The Red Sox had Yankees right-hander Vic Raschi, a 21-game winner who allowed a .241 average against him.

That morning, Kell remembered, his wife Charlene called Tiger Stadium and asked to be patched through to the clubhouse.

"You're going to lead the league in hitting," she confidently told her husband. "I know you can. All you need is a couple of hits."

Kell relayed the conversation to his friend Hoot Evers, then said, "What if Williams goes out and gets four?"

Williams had 37 career games with four or more hits, but the game on October 2, 1949, was not one of them. He went 0 for 2 with two walks against Raschi, dropping his average a point to .343.

And Kell got his two hits.

He doubled off Lemon in the first inning, singled in

When the writers voted for the Hall of Fame, Kell never got more than 36.8 percent.

the third, and walked in the sixth. The Indians, trying to finish in third place, brought Bob Feller in from the bullpen. Kell flied out against Feller in the seventh, leaving him at .343.

Or, more precisely, at .342912.

The Red Sox game finished when the Tigers were still in the ninth inning. Williams had finished the season at .342756.

If Kell didn't make another out, he would win the batting title by the slimmest of margins. The only problem: he was the fourth scheduled Tiger batter in the ninth inning.

Dick Wakefield's one-out pinch single off Feller meant Kell's spot was likely to come up. As Kell told the story later, Joe Ginsberg was yelling at him from the Tiger dugout as Eddie Lake stepped to the plate. The Tigers had found out that the Red Sox game was over, and manager Red Rolfe was going to have Ginsberg hit for Kell to protect his lead.

Before Kell even realized what was happening, Lake hit a ground ball to Ray Boone. Boone stepped on the bag and threw to first to end the game and the Tigers' season, and to give Kell the batting title that would be the greatest individual achievement of his 15-year career.

Who knows, but it may have even been what would eventually put him in the Hall of Fame.

THE 1949 BATTING RACE, MONTH BY MONTH

	APRIL
Kell .348	
Williams .306	

	MAY
Kell .335	
Williams .333	

	JUNE
Kell .353	
Williams .320	

	JULY
Kell .341	
Williams .340	

	AUGUST
Williams .356	
Kell .340	

	SEPTEMBER
Williams .344	
Kell .340	

	OCTOBER 2 (end of season)
Kell .3429	
Williams .3428	

To a later generation of Tiger fans, Kell would become best-known as the voice of the Tigers on television (and as Al Kaline's broadcast partner). Kell also played a part in bringing Ernie Harwell to Detroit from Baltimore.

As the years went by, his playing career would be more and more overlooked. Kell was an outstanding player, a 10-time All-Star, but there were always those who got more attention. When the writers voted for the Hall of Fame, Kell never got more than 36.8 percent. He eventually got in through the veterans' committee.

He was proud of his career, and especially of his seven seasons with the Tigers, but he never put himself on the level of Williams, who he called "the best hitter I ever saw."

For one memorable season and especially on one memorable final day, George Kell outdid Ted Williams. And of all the batting titles Tiger players have won, that one might have been as meaningful as any.

Rudy York's

18

Homer Month

Rudy York hit one home run in April 1937, none in May, and three in June.

And 18 in August.

He started the season as a rookie third baseman who batted seventh and couldn't stay in the lineup. He ended it as the catcher who broke Babe Ruth's record—and held on to it for 61 years.

Even now, only one player in baseball history has hit more home runs in a month than York did in August 1937. Sammy Sosa hit 20 in June 1998, at the height of baseball's steroid era.

Barry Bonds, even with steroids, never had a month like York's. Neither did Mark McGwire, Mickey Mantle, Roger Maris, Hank Aaron, or even the Babe himself.

Aaron hit 755 home runs, but never more than 12 in any one month. York hit 277 in his career—he's 167th on the all-time list, just behind

Mike Cameron and Ryan Klesko—but there was that one month where he hit 18.

And another where he hit 17, because York nearly tied his own record six years later, in August 1943.

You wonder how that could happen, but you wonder how a lot of Rudy York's career could happen. You also wonder how York may have done had he come along in a different era, say one where he could have been a designated hitter.

As it was, he moved from catcher to third base to the outfield and finally to first base, after the Tigers paid Hank Greenberg a bonus to get Greenberg to move to the outfield instead.

No matter where York played, he was a bad fielder who played only because he could hit.

"He was too awkward at third, too heavy-footed for the outfield, too wild as a pitcher, and too immobile for a good catcher," the Associated Press wrote in York's 1970 obituary.

The Tigers signed York in 1933, and sent him to their Shreveport farm team as a 19-year-old second baseman. He moved around, from team to team and position to position, playing three games with the Tigers in 1934 but landing back in the minors for the next two seasons. His defense was too shaky, and the Tiger teams of the mid-1930s were too loaded with talent. York hit 32 home runs at Beaumont in 1935 and 37 home runs at Milwaukee in 1936, but it wasn't until 1937 that the Tigers gave him a chance to stick in the majors.

York wanted to play first base, but Greenberg wasn't ready to move.

"We're going to shift [York] around until we find a place for him," manager Mickey Cochrane told reporters.

York landed at third base, but two weeks into the season Cochrane was regularly playing Marv Owen there and leaving York on the bench. It wasn't until the middle of June that York found his way into the everyday lineup.

MOST HOME RUNS IN A MONTH, TIGERS

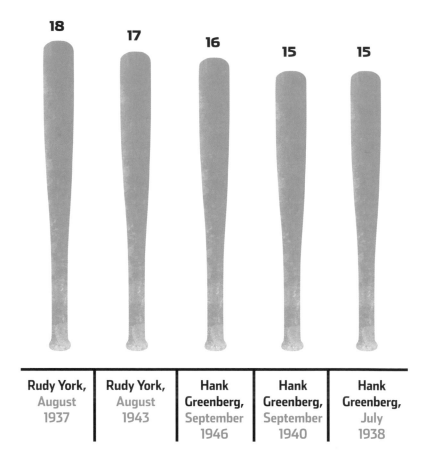

18	17	16	15	15
Rudy York, August 1937	**Rudy York,** August 1943	**Hank Greenberg,** September 1946	**Hank Greenberg,** September 1940	**Hank Greenberg,** July 1938

Reports from the time suggest that York was something of a disaster at third base, but his power kept him in the lineup. He homered eight times and drove in 27 runs in 19 games in July. Finally, four games into August, with Birdie Tebbetts struggling, Cochrane decided to make York the Tiger catcher.

York said he didn't like catching, but he did like playing. He responded to the new job by hitting three home runs in the next four games. He kept playing, and the home runs kept coming.

He hit his 16th of the month on August 30 against the Yankees, coming within one of tying Ruth's eight-year-old record. The next day against Washington, York went 4 for 4 with two home runs and seven RBIs.

He ended August with 18 homers but also with 50 RBIs, in 30 games. The RBI total is still tied for the third most any major leaguer has ever had in a month, behind the record 53 set by Hack Wilson in August 1930 and tied by Joe DiMaggio in August 1939.

York followed up his 18-homer August by hitting just three in September. He finished the 1937 season with 35 home runs, good for fifth in the American League. He played eight more seasons with the Tigers and even won a home run title, when he hit 34 in the war year of 1943.

In 1938, *Newsweek* put York on the cover, with a headline that read: "Rudy York: greatest slugger since Babe Ruth?" But York never lived up to that hype. He stayed with the Tigers until January 1946, when they needed to make room for Greenberg to move back to first base and traded York to the Red Sox.

He played with the Red Sox, White Sox, and A's, and even went back to the minor leagues and to semipro ball when his time in the major leagues was done. The AP obituary said he was working as a painter when he died of lung cancer at age 56.

York would hold on to his big-league record for 28 more years. He still holds the American League record for most homers in a month.

You look at it, and you still wonder how it happened. You still wonder what might have been.

Hank Greenberg's

183

RBIs in 1937

Hank Greenberg is a lot better known for hitting 58 home runs in 1938 than he is for driving in 183 runs the year before.

But he shouldn't be.

For one thing, Greenberg himself always maintained that the 1937 season was the best of his career. For another, his 183 RBIs have stood the test of time better than his 58 home runs.

Since Greenberg hit 58 home runs, seven sluggers have topped it and two others have equaled it. Admittedly, many were steroid-aided, but the fact is, 58 home runs no longer sounds anything close to impossible.

The way 183 RBIs does.

In 77 years of baseball since Greenberg drove in 183, no one else has matched it. It was the third-highest total when he did it (behind

HANK GREENBERG'S BIGGEST RBI SEASONS

183*	170*	150*	146	139
1937	1935	1940	1938	1934

*Led league

Hack Wilson's 191 and Lou Gehrig's 185), and it's still the third-highest total today.

In fact, in the last 77 years, even with expansion and 162-game schedules and steroids and amphetamines and corked bats, no one has come within 15 RBIs of Greenberg's 183. Only one player has even come within 20 (Manny Ramirez in 1999, with 165).

Yes, baseball was a high-scoring game in the late 1930s. American League teams averaged 5.2 runs a game in 1937. But that's no different from the height of the steroid era (AL teams averaged 5.2 runs a game in 1999, too), and yet no one was driving in 183 runs—or even 170.

No Tiger since Greenberg has come within 40 RBIs of matching his club record. Rocky Colavito drove in 140 in 1961, and Miguel Cabrera had 139 in his Triple Crown season of 2012. Cabrera could have played 50 more games driving in runs at the same rate, and he still wouldn't have caught Greenberg.

Greenberg still owns the top four RBI totals in Tiger history, numbers he took much more pride in than his 58 home runs (which also remains the club record).

"I've always believed that the most important aspect of hitting is driving in runs," Greenberg told Lawrence Ritter in *The Glory of Their Times.* "Runs batted in are more important than batting average, more important than home runs, more important than anything. That's what wins ballgames: driving runs across the plate."

Greenberg told of how he would always yell to teammate Charlie Gehringer that he just needed a runner moved from first to third.

"I'll get him in," Greenberg would say.

A lot more often than not, he did.

Greenberg understood the appeal of the home run. He understood baseball fans' desire to identify "the next Babe Ruth," and Jewish fans' desire to anoint him as "the Jewish Babe Ruth."

For years, many wanted to believe that the only reason Greenberg didn't get to 60 home runs and match or beat the Babe's record was that opposing pitchers didn't want a Jew to be the one to break it.

Greenberg's biographer, Mark Kurlansky, largely debunks that legend in his book *Hank Greenberg: The Hero Who Didn't Want to Be One.*

"There is no evidence of conspiracy against Greenberg," Kurlansky wrote, adding that Greenberg always maintained that he got more than his share of breaks and that he believed fans were rooting for him to break the record.

Greenberg himself told Ritter that the legend was "pure baloney.... The reason I didn't hit 60 or 61 is because I ran out of gas; it had nothing to do with being Jewish."

Greenberg's Jewish heritage did play in to who he was, and to his place in the Detroit community in a difficult era. And it led to perhaps the best story about his pursuit of 60 home runs.

When the chase was on (Greenberg had 37 home runs by the end of July, and he hit his 58th with five games remaining), Greenberg's mother told him that if he broke the record, she'd celebrate by making him 61 gefilte fish in the shape of baseballs.

"It's just as well," Greenberg said after he fell three homers short. "There is no way I could have eaten all that gefilte fish."

Hank Greenberg stands in front of the dugout in Briggs Stadium in 1937. *(Mark Rucker)*

HANK GREENBERG'S 58 HOME RUNS IN 1938

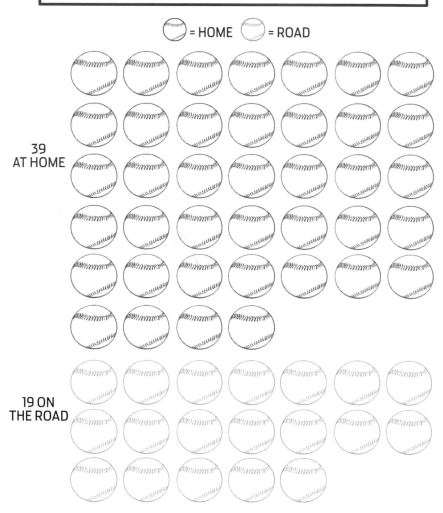

⚾ = HOME   ⚾ = ROAD

39 AT HOME

19 ON THE ROAD

Perhaps it's just as well that the 183 RBIs didn't get as much attention.

No matter what, Greenberg goes down as one of the best players in Tiger history, one of the best in baseball history. Not bad for a guy who only became a Tiger because of Lou Gehrig, and because he came of age two decades before the founding of the NBA.

Basketball was Greenberg's first love, and he thought it was his better sport in high school in New York. But there was nowhere to make money playing the game then, and the Yankees were offering him $10,000 to sign with them.

Greenberg turned that down, figuring there was no way he was going to unseat Gehrig at first base, and later accepted $1,000 less to sign with the Tigers (after scout Jean Dubuc pleased his parents by saying that $6,000 of the $9,000 bonus would be paid after he first went to college at New York University).

The irony is that when Greenberg got to the major leagues with the Tigers in 1933, manager Bucky Harris tried to turn him into a third baseman (after buying first baseman Harry Davis for $75,000). The third base experiment didn't last, but seven years later the Tigers would ask Greenberg to move to left field so that Rudy York could play first base.

Greenberg moved, and was so unbothered by it that he had league-leading totals of 50 doubles and 41 home runs that year and was named baseball's Most Valuable Player.

Oh, and Greenberg drove in 150 runs in that 1940 season, too. We mustn't forget that.

"Runs batted in were my obsession, not home runs," Greenberg always said.

And with 183 of them in 1937, RBIs are really how Hank Greenberg should be remembered.

Charlie Gehringer's

60

Doubles in 1936

They called Charlie Gehringer the "Mechanical Man" when he played for the Tigers. It was a tribute to his consistency, but also to his personality. Plenty of players from those early Tiger teams sound like they would have been fascinating to talk to, great subjects to get to know and write about.

Gehringer was not one of them.

He was a great player, a Hall of Famer, "the greatest second baseman who ever lived," in the eyes of teammate and fellow Hall of Famer Hank Greenberg. He just wasn't all that thrilling in conversation.

In fact, legend has it that Gehringer almost never spoke at all.

"You can't talk your way into a batting championship," he once explained.

Or a doubles crown, for that matter.

Gehringer won one batting title. He led the league in doubles twice, and the second time he did it, he put up a number that still hasn't been matched.

Sixty doubles isn't a major league record for a season. It wasn't even the most in the major leagues that season. Joe Medwick had 64 for the Cardinals.

It isn't even a Tigers franchise record. Greenberg had 63 in 1934.

But even though Gehringer's total wasn't the most in the majors in 1936, it's still more than anyone has had in the major leagues *since* 1936.

CHARLIE GEHRINGER'S TOP DOUBLES SEASONS

1936 ▸ **60***

1934 ▸ **50**

1930 ▸ **47**

1929 ▸ **45***

1932 ▸ **44**

*Led league

We're going on 80 years now, and no one has matched what Gehringer did for the Tigers that season.

As Lefty Gomez once said, "Every time I turn around, the guy's on second base."

Gehringer actually had better seasons than he did in '36. He was named the MVP the next year, when he won the batting title. He had a career-high OPS-plus of 149 (meaning 49 percent better than average) in 1934, the year the Tigers won their first American League pennant since 1909.

They won their first World Series title the year after that, with Gehringer teaming with Greenberg and Goose Goslin to make "G-Men" part of everyday speech for a generation of Tiger fans.

Gehringer had been one of those fans himself, born in 1903 (just two years after the Tigers became a charter member of the American League) in Fowlerville, Michigan. He kept a scrapbook of newspaper clippings about the Tigers of the Ty Cobb era.

He was a pitcher in high school, and actually thought about pitching in pro ball, as well. He played football, basketball, and baseball at the University of Michigan, not sure that he'd make a living as a player but thinking he might be a coach or P.E. teacher.

No one is quite sure how he ended up signing with the Tigers, but one story is that Tigers outfielder Bobby Veach saw him play while on a hunting trip near Fowlerville. Another is that a friend of Veach's arranged a tryout for Gehringer in Detroit.

However it happened, Gehringer showed up in Detroit at age 20, signed a contract for a $300 bonus, and went on to become one of the best players in the history of the franchise. He played a handful of big-league games in 1924 and 1925, but got his big break the next year, when starting second baseman Frank O'Rourke came down with the measles.

"Frank got sick, I went to second, and I stayed there for quite a while," Gehringer would say, years later.

MOST DOUBLES IN A SEASON, TIGERS

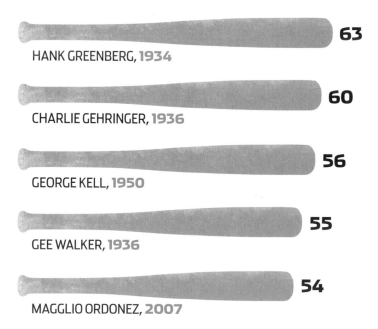

HANK GREENBERG, **1934** — 63

CHARLIE GEHRINGER, **1936** — 60

GEORGE KELL, **1950** — 56

GEE WALKER, **1936** — 55

MAGGLIO ORDONEZ, **2007** — 54

Quite a while, as in the next 15 years.

As Doc Cramer once said, "All you have to do is wind him up on Opening Day and he runs on and on, doing everything right."

Gehringer hit some home runs. He led the league in triples and stolen bases one year. He drove in more than 100 runs seven times.

But if he had to be known for one thing offensively, it was for all the doubles. He led the league with 45 doubles in 1929, and he topped 40 seven times in a nine-year span.

The 1936 season was a difficult one in some ways. The Tigers had been to back-to-back World Series, but in April of 1936, Greenberg broke his wrist (the same one he broke in the 1935 World Series) in a baseline collision with Washington's Jake Powell. Mickey Cochrane, the player/manager who had turned the Tigers into champions, was limited to 44 games and suffered a nervous breakdown. General Crowder, a 16-game winner the year before, had a stomach problem that forced him to retire.

The Tigers still finished second in the American League, but it was a distant second, behind a revived Yankee team that featured MVP Lou Gehrig and a standout rookie named Joe DiMaggio.

In a decade in which the Tigers became champions, the 1936 season wasn't memorable—except for Gehringer's 60 doubles. He had 26 of them in the final 57 games of the season to beat teammate Gee Walker, who was second in the league with 55.

Gehringer would never come close to 60 doubles again. No Tiger would come close until 1950, when George Kell had 56, and no one after that until 2007, when Magglio Ordonez had 54.

And no one with any other team would get to 60, either.

No one has matched the Mechanical Man.

Harry Heilmann's

4

Batting Titles

Ty Cobb's biggest contributions to the Tigers came with his bat, and with his legs. He could hit and he could run, and he did enough of both that he's remembered as one of the best players ever, maybe the best ever.

But is there any other Hall of Famer who also gets credit for scouting a Hall of Famer? Is there any other Hall of Famer who also gets credit for coaching a Hall of Famer?

Is there anything else in baseball history like the story of Ty Cobb and Harry Heilmann?

Heilmann was without doubt a great player. His .342 career batting average is the third-best ever for a right-handed hitter, behind only Rogers Hornsby and Ed Delahanty. He was the biggest Tigers star in the 1920s, and then he was the voice of the Tigers for many on radio through the 1930s and '40s.

And since Heilmann started George Kell on the way to Kell's own broadcasting career, you could make the case that Heilmann influenced Tiger fans all the way into the 1990s.

Now, can you make the case that it was Cobb who brought Heilmann to the Tigers, or that it was Cobb who made Heilmann into a batting champ?

What is known for sure is that Heilmann didn't play baseball in high school in San Francisco, and that he was an 18-year-old bookkeeper for the Mutual Biscuit Company when he agreed to play in a semipro game for $10. A scout saw him, he ended up in Portland playing in the Northwestern League, and before long league president Fielder Jones recommended Heilmann to the Tigers, who drafted him in September 1913.

The story Cobb told is that Jones called him about Heilmann, and that Cobb himself went to San Francisco in the off-season "and tested him long and hard." Cobb told biographer Al Stump that Heilmann's father didn't want his son to go to the Tigers, but that "finally I convinced him that we didn't want Harry to join a bank-robbery gang back east."

However it really happened, the fact is that Heilmann was a decent player when he came to Detroit...and a great one after Cobb succeeded Hughie Jennings as the Tiger manager in 1921. Heilmann hit .394 to win the batting title that year—just ahead of Cobb (.389), who was player/manager. He hit .403 two years later to win the crown again, and .393 two years after that to win it a third time. Sure enough, two years after that, in 1927, Heilmann batted .398 and won his fourth crown.

The fact is that Heilmann had a .291 career average while Jennings was the Tiger manager, and a .377 average while Cobb was in charge.

Cobb said he offered to give Heilmann some of his bats when they were simply teammates, but that Heilmann refused. By 1921, though, Heilmann was taking Cobb's suggestions (or Cobb was finally offering them), and the results were obvious.

The Heilmann-Cobb batting race was a close one, so close that it came down to the final day of the season—and beyond. Heilmann went 1 for 4 in the last game; Cobb didn't play, as he was serving a league-imposed suspension. The newspapers, relying on unofficial tabulations, listed the final numbers as Cobb .391, Heilmann .390.

HARRY HEILMANN'S BATTING TITLES

1921 ▶ **.394**

1923 ▶ **.403**

1925 ▶ **.393**

1927 ▶ **.398**

Heilmann offered his congratulations to Cobb, telling him "the better man won." It wasn't until two months later that the official statistics came out. Heilmann had actually batted .394, Cobb .389. Heilmann had ended Cobb's 14-year run as the Tigers' top hitter. He also became the first right-handed hitter in 16 years to win the AL batting crown.

Cobb was gracious in public, but a mutual friend told Heilmann that his manager had actually called the official statisticians to tell them their numbers had to be wrong.

Heilmann won the 1923 race more easily, finishing 10 points ahead of Babe Ruth (and finishing behind only Ruth in on-base, slugging, and WAR). He became the only Tiger other than Cobb to ever hit .400 in a season, a distinction he still holds today.

In 1925, Heilmann trailed Tris Speaker by 24 points in mid-September. Speaker was hurting and didn't play much that month. Heilmann, meanwhile, had 46 hits in his final 83 at-bats, a .554 run that raised his average from .365 to .393. He went 6 for 9 in a doubleheader on the final day, moving from one point behind Speaker to four points in front.

Speaker didn't play that final day, so when Heilmann had three hits in the first game, he had moved percentage points ahead. Told he could win the title by sitting out the second game, Heilmann responded, "Not me. I'll win it fairly, or not at all. I'll be in there swinging."

Neither Heilmann nor Cobb won the 1926 batting race, but Heinie Manush did. He was another player recommended to the Tigers by Cobb, another Cobb pupil.

"If I went without a hit on Friday, he wouldn't speak to me on Saturday," Manush would say later. "I couldn't like him as a man, no way. He ran things like a dictator. But as a teacher—well, he was the best."

The 1927 batting race was tight all the way down the stretch, but by the final day, Heilmann's .391 average left him five points ahead of runner-up Al Simmons. Again, Heilmann refused to sit out. Again, he had a huge final day, going 7 for 9 in a doubleheader against the Cleveland Indians to raise his average to .398 and wrap up the Tigers' 17th batting title in 21 seasons.

By 1927, Cobb was already gone from the Tigers. Two years later, Heilmann would also leave, sold to the Cincinnati Reds in part because he and new manager Bucky Harris didn't see eye to eye.

The Tigers would go another decade before Charlie Gehringer won their next batting title, in 1937. No Tiger would again win multiple titles until Miguel Cabrera arrived and won three in a row.

By then, the man they called "Slug" would have his name listed with the Tigers' other Hall of Famers on the back wall at Comerica Park. Heilmann died in 1951, nearly half a century before the new park opened, but he remains one of the best players the Tigers ever had.

All thanks (perhaps) to Ty Cobb.

Ty Cobb's

5

Homer Spree

The year Ty Cobb debuted with the Tigers, it took eight home runs to lead the American League. The year he retired, it took 54.

Baseball changed drastically in Cobb's 24 seasons. Cobb spurred some of that change, but he also resisted it. He resisted any thought that hitting home runs made you king.

Cobb hated Babe Ruth. He regularly insulted Babe Ruth. He fought with the Babe for the country's attention and respect. He always wanted to be paid more than the Babe.

Eventually, there was a day when he fought with the Babe—literally—on the field.

But there was also one two-day span where Ty Cobb gave in to the lure of power. Or, if you prefer, proved his point.

It was in May 1925, in St. Louis, and two writers approached Cobb for an interview. As Cobb's biographer Al Stump told the story,

Cobb turned to them and said: "I'm surprised you boys want to talk to me, since you're so impressed by the home run."

Then Cobb, who never hit more than 12 home runs in a season, told the writers something else.

"Gentlemen, pay close attention," he said. "I'll show you something new. For the first time in my life, I will be deliberately going for home runs. For years I've been reading comparisons about how others hit, as against my style. So I'm going to give you a demonstration."

And he did, with one of the most spectacular two-day displays in baseball history.

He hit a two-run home run off Bullet Joe Bush in the first inning. He hit another two-run home run off Elam Vangilder, this one over the pavilion and completely out of the ballpark, in the second inning. He hit a solo home run off Milt Gaston in the eighth. He also had two doubles and a single. Cobb finished the day 6 for 6 with five RBIs and 16 total bases.

He wasn't done.

Cobb came back the next day and hit a two-run homer off Dave Danforth in the fifth inning. And a three-run homer off Chet Falk in the ninth. He went 3 for 6 that day, with six RBIs.

In all, Cobb hit five home runs in two days, something that at that point in his career Ruth had never done—something Ruth would never do.

MOST TOTAL BASES IN A GAME, TIGERS

16
Ty Cobb,
5-5-1925
at Browns

15
Dmitri Young,
5-6-2003
at Orioles

13
nine
players

No player to that point had ever homered five times in two back-to-back games. No other player would do it for another 11 years, and even now, no player has topped it.

It's the one major league home run record that Ty Cobb ever set, the only one he even wanted.

Cobb's 16 total bases in one game were also a record, one no one in the American League topped until Josh Hamilton had 18 in a 2012 four-homer performance in Baltimore.

Cobb finished the day 6 for 6 with five RBIs and 16 total bases.

The two-day spree didn't change Cobb. He hit only seven more home runs the rest of that 1925 season, only 17 more over the final 3½ seasons of his career. He played 418 more games in his career, and hit two home runs in only one of them—on May 9, 1926, at Yankee Stadium, in a game where Ruth didn't hit a home run.

The two-day spree didn't change baseball, either. Two years later, the Babe hit 60. The home run never did go out of style. If Cobb was trying to make the point that hitting home runs wasn't that difficult, and that they shouldn't be celebrated, then he failed.

He did, however, leave us with a question we'll never be able to answer: How many home runs could Ty Cobb have hit?

We'll never know for sure, but on the evidence of those two days in St. Louis when he did try, the answer may well have been: As many as he wanted to.

Aloysius Travers Allows

24

Runs in One Game

The year John Hiller set what was then the major league record for saves in a season, he pitched 125⅓ innings and allowed 21 runs.

The day Aloysius Travers set a major league record that still stands, he pitched eight innings and allowed 24 runs.

In one game.

It was in 1912, so there's no pitch count available. Not that anyone would have cared, because Al Travers never pitched again. Then again, he'd never pitched before, either.

He wasn't a pitcher. He wasn't a baseball player, except on that one strange day in Philadelphia when the real Tiger players went on strike to protest Ty Cobb's suspension.

And Aloysius Travers walked into history.

He would later be ordained as a Catholic priest, but on that day Travers was a 20-year-old student at St. Joseph's University. He was the assistant student manager for the St. Joe's baseball team, and he had come to know *Philadelphia Bulletin* sportswriter Joe Nolan.

Nolan knew Tiger manager Hughie Jennings, and with Jennings' players threatening a strike (and with American League president Ban Johnson threatening a $5,000 fine), Jennings asked Nolan for help lining up replacement players. Nolan asked Travers, who rounded up some friends for the May 18 game at Shibe Park.

And when Travers found out that the pitcher would be paid $50 (double what the other replacements would get), he became a pitcher.

He would say later that he never really expected the game to be played.

"We thought we'd just go out and appear," Travers told Red Smith. "We never thought we'd play a game."

They not only played a game, they faced a Philadelphia A's team that won the World Series the year before and would win 90 games in 1912. They faced a pair of Hall of Fame infielders, Frank "Home Run" Baker and Eddie Collins.

> *They not only played a game, they faced a Philadelphia A's team that won the World Series the year before and would win 90 games in 1912.*

It's as if you took a random kid from Wayne State and asked him to pitch to Miguel Cabrera and Victor Martinez.

Think of it that way, and it's amazing that Travers gave up *only* 24 runs. It's amazing the rag-tag bunch of substitute Tigers scored two.

"I was throwing slow curves and the A's weren't used to them and couldn't hit the ball," Travers told Smith. "Hughie Jennings told me not to throw fastballs as he was afraid I might get killed. I was doing fine until they started bunting. The guy playing third base had never played baseball before.

"I threw a beautiful slow ball and the A's were just hitting easy flies. Trouble was, no one could catch them."

The 20-year-old Travers pitched to 48-year-old catcher Deacon Jim McGuire, a Tigers coach. The third baseman he mentioned was boxer Billy Maharg, who later helped fix the 1919 World Series. The center fielder was Bill Leinhauser, who supposedly got hit by his wife with a skillet when she found out he played in place of Cobb.

Travers is still there, with his 0-1 record and 15.75 ERA, his eight innings pitched, seven walks, and one strikeout (by A's shortstop Jack Barry).

The whole farce came about because Cobb went into the stands in New York three days earlier to confront—and fight—a heckler who allegedly insulted his mother and his sister and just wouldn't shut up. The heckler had lost his fingers as a result of a printing press accident, which brought on a memorable exchange.

"He has no hands!" fans yelled at Cobb.

"I don't care if he has no legs," Cobb was said to have replied.

In any case, Johnson happened to be at the game, and suspended Cobb indefinitely. Cobb's teammates hated him, but decided that at least this one time, Cobb was in the right.

"Feeling that Mr. Cobb is being done a grave injustice, we, the undersigned, refuse to play another game until such action is adjusted to our satisfaction," they wrote, in a letter to Johnson.

It took just the one crazy game in Philadelphia for Johnson to act. He canceled the next game, reduced Cobb's suspension to 10 days and a $50 fine, and fined the other striking Tigers $100 apiece. Cobb later claimed that Johnson backed down when he threatened to sue the league for $100,000.

Cobb would go on to hit .409 that year, winning his sixth consecutive AL batting title. Travers would go back to his studies.

But years later, when any Tiger pitcher had a really bad day, a trip back through the record book would turn up the name of Aloysius Travers.

He's still there, still in that Tigers record book, still in that major league record book. A century later, no other Tiger pitcher has allowed 24 runs in a game, no other Tiger pitcher has allowed 26 hits in a game, and no other Tiger pitcher has allowed seven triples in a game.

Travers is still there, with his 0–1 record and 15.75 ERA, his eight innings pitched, seven walks, and one strikeout (by A's shortstop Jack Barry).

In the last half-century, no pitcher has ever been left in a game to allow more than 14 runs (Vin Mazzaro of the Royals did that in 2011). It's hard to believe any pitcher again ever would.

So on the list of records that won't be broken, perhaps Aloysius Travers' place is safe.

Mike Maroth Loses

21

Games in 2003

It has been 12 years, and it still comes up, every now and then. Mike Maroth still gets recognized, still gets asked about that season.

"Not very often," Maroth said. "And most of the time, people give me positive comments."

It has been 12 years, and we can say with some certainty now that losing 20 games in a season didn't destroy Mike Maroth's life or career, no matter how much consternation and conversation there was back in 2003. Maroth remains the last big-league pitcher to lose 20, the only big-league pitcher in 34 years to lose 20, but it's more a footnote than a long-lasting stigma.

Maroth never wanted to be Brian Kingman, who loved being the last guy (before Maroth) to lose 20. Maroth never ran from his history, but he never wanted it to define who he is or even who he was.

He came to terms early with what that 2003 season meant, understood that the 9–21 record was as reflective of the bad team he played for as it was of anything he did on the mound.

"I felt good about never quitting," Maroth said, 11 years on from 2003. "I wasn't going to give in. I wanted to go out there and help my team any way I could, and I felt I accomplished that."

> **Maroth went on to pitch in the big leagues for four more seasons, with nearly as many wins (35) as losses (36).**

He went on to pitch in the big leagues for four more seasons, with nearly as many wins (35) as losses (36). His playing career ended not because of any residual effects from 2003, but from elbow problems and shoulder problems and knee problems.

"Injuries were really my roadblock," he said.

He's a minor-league pitching coach now, back in the Tiger organization, hopeful he's on a path that leads back to the big leagues as a coach. He has something to offer the young pitchers he works with, the experience of pitching in the major leagues and the experience of facing adversity and continuing to fight.

There's a toughness inside that isn't always evident the first time you meet Maroth, who first came to the Tigers as a 21-year-old minor-leaguer in a July deadline deal that sent Bryce Florie to the Boston Red Sox. There's a determination that showed up in that 2003 season, Maroth's first full year in the major leagues.

He showed promise in 21 big-league starts the year before, enough that he was named the 25-year-old Opening Day starter for a Tiger team that was overmatched right from the start. Maroth allowed just two runs in seven innings on Opening Day, but all he got for it was an 0–1 record.

A month later, Maroth carried a no-hitter into the eighth inning against the Baltimore Orioles. His reward was another loss, which left him 0–7 on May 1.

He was 1–10 by the end of May, 5–15 by the end of July. Much of the talk by then was whether the Tigers would lose 120 games to match the 1962 New York Mets, but already people were also asking whether Maroth or Jeremy Bonderman might become the first pitcher in 23 years to lose 20.

Bonderman was just 20 years old, and the Tigers took steps to make sure he wouldn't lose more than 19, pulling him from the starting rotation. But Maroth went on.

He lost his 19th game on August 30, and he took the mound and lost again five nights later in Toronto, even though he found out just before the game that his grandmother had died.

"I'm a strong person," he said that night. "I'm going to overcome this."

It wasn't until that winter that it all sunk in, that he accepted the idea that there was honor in going on and that he could take pride in refusing to quit. Maroth remained in the rotation even after losing 20, making four more starts before the season ended.

He lost one more game, his 21st, but he also won three more, including a win on the final day of the season to save the Tigers from losing 120.

In the 1970s alone, 15 pitchers lost 20 or more in a season (including Mickey Lolich with the 1974 Tigers).

"Looking back, would I change anything I did? No," Maroth said. "I would have liked to have done better, to change the results. But I wouldn't change what I did."

If you see him now and you want to bring up 2003, go ahead. If you want to ask about the rest of his career, that's even better.

And when another pitcher someday is going for a 20th loss, Mike Maroth will be ready for the phone calls. He knows they'll come. He won't hide from them, any more than he would have hidden in 2003.

He's not the next Brian Kingman. Kingman went 8–20 in 1980, at a time when losing 20 wasn't really a big deal. In the 1970s alone, 14 pitchers lost 20 or more in a season (including Mickey Lolich with the 1974 Tigers).

But Kingman was the last before Maroth, and as the years went on he became more and more protective of the title. He didn't want another pitcher to take it away, and he would even travel to the games when a pitcher with 19 losses was starting again.

"I'm sure people will call, and I'll talk to them," Maroth said. "I'm not going to the games. That's not me."

He doesn't need it to be. He's not ashamed to have lost 21 games in a season, but he's not hanging on to it, either.

"Losing 21 games is not an accomplishment," Maroth said.

It's not an accomplishment, but it's not a problem.

It doesn't define him. It didn't destroy him.

It's been 11 years, and Mike Maroth is just fine.

Tigers Lose

119

(But Not 120) in 2003

Most teams end the season in disappointment. It's just the way baseball is. You're disappointed that you didn't make the playoffs, or you're disappointed that you lost in October.

One team wins, and the rest wish they did.

Almost no one ends the season with smiles, but the 2003 Tigers did. They lost more games than any team in franchise history—more games than any team in American League history...

But they didn't lose 120.

It was all anyone was talking about, and not just in the final days of the season. The Tigers were coming off a 106-loss 2002 season, and despite bringing the popular Alan Trammell back as manager, they had made few moves to make anyone think 2003 would be better. So when the Tigers began the season 0–9, and then 1–17, it didn't take long for people to start bringing up the 1962 Mets.

The '62 Mets, the Tigers heard, almost every day. The '62 Mets, and 120 losses, and are you going to end up with 120, too?

They nearly did.

From September 5 to September 22, the Tigers lost 16 out of 17. They were 38–118, and they still had six games left to play.

They had to win five of six. They hadn't won five of six all year. Heck, there were only three times all year they'd even won four of six.

> **From September 5 to September 22, the Tigers lost**
>
> **15 out of 16.**

There was no way they'd avoid losing 120—and somewhere on a long-lost computer disk, I've got a story that says they didn't avoid it.

This was big news, and Booth Newspapers had told me that the story of the 120th loss was going on page A-1. When the Tigers fell behind the Minnesota Twins 8–0 on the final Saturday night of the season, I had to get that story ready.

It never ran. As he did all that final weekend, Twins manager Ron Gardenhire pulled his starters (including pitcher Brad Radke) out of the game after the fifth inning. It wasn't a sympathy move. Gardenhire was simply getting the division champion Twins ready for the playoffs, and there was no sense in wearing anyone out.

The Tigers scored three times in the seventh, and tied the game with four in the eighth. They won it 9–8 when Alex Sanchez came home on a Jesse Orosco wild pitch in the ninth, and suddenly all they needed to avoid 120 was one simple win.

No problem. They'd won games before, 42 times. So what if they'd also lost 119.

On the final day of the season, Gardenhire didn't even start many of his regulars. Starting pitcher Kyle Lohse went just three innings, tuning up for his Game 3 playoff start against the Yankees.

It was a 2–2 game through five, before the Tigers scored seven times in the sixth inning. It was their biggest inning of the entire season.

The final was 9–4. Mike Maroth, who earlier in September had become the first pitcher in 23 years to lose 20 games in a season, got credit for the final win, his team-leading ninth of the year.

LOSINGEST TIGER SEASONS

2003 ▶ **43-119**

1996 ▶ **53-109**

2002 ▶ **55-109**

1952 ▶ **50-104**

1989 ▶ **59-103**

And when reporters got to the clubhouse, the Tigers were celebrating. General manager Dave Dombrowski was going from locker to locker shaking every player's hand.

"We're the happiest worst team ever," Matt Anderson yelled, as his teammates cheered.

It's still one of my favorite quotes ever.

The '62 Mets were safe as the only 120-loss team ever, and as Bobby Higginson told reporters that day, it was just as well.

"You know, to be honest with you, it just has a ring," Higginson said. "The '62 Mets just has a ring, as compared to the '03 Tigers. That just doesn't sound right."

Trammell, the first-year manager who left the team early in that final week to attend his mother's funeral, chose to focus on the way his overmatched team played hard all the way to the end of such a difficult season. He and his players talked about how going through a year like this could only make them better, and how it would make the wins to come that much sweeter.

For some of the 2003 Tigers, those thoughts came true.

Of the 43 players who appeared in a game in 2003, 12 hung around long enough to play for the 2006 team that went to the World Series (nine of them were on the World Series roster). Three others (Andres Torres, Cody Ross, and Carlos Pena) would go on to make the World Series with other teams.

Then again, 11 of the 2003 Tigers never played in the major leagues again.

It was a bad team, a team fully deserving of being remembered as the worst Tiger team ever.

Just remember, they were also the happiest worst team ever.

The

12

Tigers Who Survived 2003 and Made It to 2006

As the awful 2003 season wore down to a close, as the Tigers worked and worked to avoid losing 120 games, they always fell back on one pleasant thought.

The bad times would make the good times to come feel that much sweeter.

It sounded nice. It also sounded unrealistic.

Who was going to believe that this band of overmatched players would ever have any good times coming?

They did. Not all of them did, but more than anyone would have thought.

When the Tigers took the field for Game 1 of the 2006 World Series, they had 2003 alum Craig Monroe in left field, 2003 alum Brandon Inge at third base, and 2003 alum Ramon Santiago at shortstop.

In all, nine of the 25 players on the Tigers' 2006 World Series roster had also been part of the team that lost 119 games three seasons before. Three other 2003 Tigers—Mike Maroth, Dmitri Young, and Chris Spurling—were part of the '06 team but didn't make it to the World Series. Young was released in early September, Spurling left on a waiver claim later that month, and Maroth was left off the postseason roster because he was coming back from an injury and just wasn't strong enough to contribute.

The rest of the 12 who survived 119 losses did contribute. Monroe hit five home runs in that postseason. Jeremy Bonderman, who lost 19 games as a 20-year-old in 2003, went $8\frac{1}{3}$ innings to win the clinching Game 4 in the Division Series against the New York Yankees. Nate Robertson pitched five shutout innings to win Game 1 of the ALCS against the Oakland A's.

Inge, who hit .203 with 30 RBIs in '03, hit 27 home runs and drove in 83 runs in '06. Jamie Walker, who was actually one of the better pitchers on the 2003 team, had a 2.81 ERA as a key left-handed reliever in 2006. Fernando Rodney had a 6.07 ERA in 2003, and a 3.52 ERA three years later.

Nine of the 25 players on the Tigers' 2006 World Series roster had also been part of the team that lost 119 games three seasons before.

Santiago was traded away in the deal that brought Carlos Guillen to the Tigers, then returned as a free agent and became a useful infielder. Omar Infante, Santiago's Opening Day double-play partner in 2003, was also a useful infielder on the 2006 team.

And Wil Ledezma, an overmatched Rule 5 pickup who had a 5.79 ERA for the 2003 team, stayed around and was useful enough to start seven games for the World Series-bound team in 2006.

The 2006 Tigers enjoyed their celebrations. All of them did. They partied after clinching a playoff spot, partied after beating the Yankees, partied after Magglio Ordonez's home run off Huston Street sent them to the World Series.

Inge, who hit .203 with 30 RBIs in 2003, hit 27 home runs and drove in 83 runs in 2006.

Some of them had more reason to celebrate than others. For some of them, the good times really did feel that much sweeter.

They knew how bad it could be. They knew how bad it had been.

They knew how far they—and the Tigers—had come.

Curtis Granderson's

23

Triples in 2007

When Comerica Park opened in 2000, baseball people took one look at its distant fences and declared it a triples paradise. And it was, at least until the Tigers shortened the outfield dimensions before the 2003 season.

With the new dimensions, Comerica went from being unquestionably the top triples park in the game to being a good to very good place to hit triples, with its spot in ESPN's park factor varying from year to year, anywhere from first in the majors to 15th.

So why did Curtis Granderson show up with the best triples season in modern major league history in 2007? And why did he actually hit more of his modern-record triples on the road than he did at home?

We're calling it a modern record, even though no one really called it that at the time. They should have, because before Granderson had his 23 triples in 2007, no one had that many in a season since 1949. No one had more triples in a season since 1925.

You can define modern however you please, but when you're the only guy in 65 years to do something, and when no one in 89 years has done any better, we're saying it should be some kind of record.

How crazy is it for a player in modern baseball to have 23 triples in a season?

Well, the very next year Granderson had only 13—and he still led the American League. No American Leaguer since has had even 15 triples (and only one National Leaguer has had 20).

And Granderson had 23.

"It was interesting how they just got contagious that year," he said a few years later. "There were ones where I'd roll over the ball and it would just get past the first baseman. And I had some lucky ones, like one that hit the wall in Cleveland and bounced away."

Granderson isn't giving himself enough credit. You get triples because you always think triple right out of the batter's box, and at that stage of his career Granderson took off every time as if he had a chance.

It helped that he was fast, although he never led the league in stolen bases. You want to say it helped that he played half his games at Comerica Park, but remember, he hit 13 of those 23 triples on the road.

MOST TRIPLES IN A SEASON, 1950–2014

23	21	21	20	20	20	20
Curtis Granderson, 2007 Tigers	Lance Johnson, 1996 Mets	Willie Wilson, 1985 Royals	Jimmy Rollins, 2007 Phillies	Cristian Guzman, 2000 Twins	George Brett, 1979 Royals	Willie Mays, 1957 Giants

Curtis Granderson dives into third base with a triple against the Brewers in June 2007 (during Verlander's first no-hitter). *(Photo Courtesy AP Photo/ Duane Burleson)*

Granderson tripled twice in Kansas City, twice in Cleveland, twice at Tampa Bay, and three times in Texas. That's three times in just two games in Texas.

"Some of those other ballparks helped," he said.

The Tigers led the major leagues in triples in 2007, but that was mostly because of Granderson. He had 23 triples. All his teammates combined had 27.

Granderson had more triples that year than four entire teams. He had more than twice as many triples as the runner-up in the American League triples race.

For Alex Rodriguez to have had that kind of gap in the 2007 AL home run race, he would have had to homer 106 times.

Granderson never had another triples year anything like 2007. He became less of a triples threat but more of a home run threat, even before the Tigers traded him to the New York Yankees (in the three-way deal that brought them Max Scherzer, among others) in December 2009.

The Yankees figured that their new ballpark would boost Granderson's home run numbers, and it did. He homered 30 times in his last season with the Tigers (with 20 of the 30 on the road), and 41 times in his second season as a Yankee (with 21 of the 41 at home).

Granderson hit 115 home runs (and just 23 triples) with the Yankees, and parlayed that into a $60 million free-agent contract with the New York Mets. The Mets were counting on some power, but they also thought that with the big outfield at their Citi Field home, Granderson might be a triples threat again.

He wasn't. He has never come close to matching the 23 he hit for the Tigers in 2007. But no one else has hit 23 since then, either.

No one else has hit 23 since 1949.

You can call it what you want. I'm calling it a modern record.

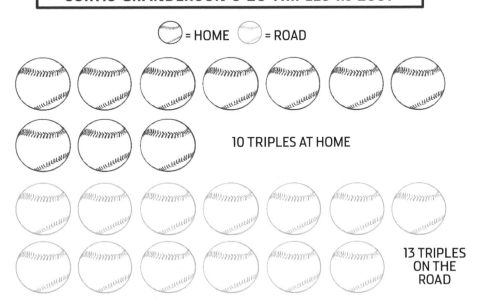

CURTIS GRANDERSON'S 23 TRIPLES IN 2007

= HOME   = ROAD

10 TRIPLES AT HOME

13 TRIPLES ON THE ROAD

Sam Crawford's

309

Triples

Baseball fans love to talk about the records that will never be broken. No one is going to top Cy Young's 511 career wins, or his 749 complete games. As the years go on, it's harder and harder to believe that anyone will catch Joe DiMaggio's streak of 56 consecutive games with a hit.

Wahoo Sam Crawford's record gets overlooked—and it shouldn't.

Wahoo Sam (and really, the nickname alone should be reason to mention him) had 309 career triples, almost all of them in his 15 seasons with the Tigers. He was the Tigers' first real star after they joined the American League, the center fielder before Ty Cobb and then the team's second star once Cobb arrived and quickly became baseball's best player.

"Crawford was a hell of a good player," Cobb later told his biographer Al Stump. "Hall of Famer. But he was only second best on our club—a bad second. He hated to be an also-ran."

At least in one category, he wasn't.

On baseball's all-time triples list, Cobb is second, with 295. Crawford is first, with 309.

It's been like that forever, or at least since Crawford topped Jake Beckley's previous record of 244 in 1913. It will be like that forever, unless baseball changes drastically.

No one is going to catch Wahoo Sam.

Only three active players have even 100 career triples. No one has more than Carl Crawford's 120, and the 33-year-old Crawford has added only eight to that total in the last three seasons.

SAM CRAWFORD'S BIGGEST TRIPLES SEASONS

1914 ▶ **26**

1903 ▶ **25**

1913 ▶ **23**

1902 ▶ **22**

1912 ▶ **21**

A 20-triple season is rarer than a 20-win season, and you know what people say about the likelihood of another pitcher getting to 300 wins.

Wahoo Sam had 20 triples in a season five times (also a major league record). Playing in an era where home runs were rare (although he once led the league with 16), Crawford was baseball's big power hitter. He led the league in triples six times, including three consecutive seasons with the 1913–15 Tigers. He also led the league in RBIs three times, with six 100-RBI seasons.

According to *The SABR Baseball List and Record Book*, Crawford also had 52 inside-the-park home runs, second in baseball history to Jesse Burkett.

Christy Mathewson was quoted as saying no batter he faced hit the ball as hard as Crawford. He was baseball's biggest slugger, who just happened to play in an era when slugging still meant having more triples than home runs.

And he had that nickname, which came to him in the simplest of ways. He hailed from Wahoo, Nebraska.

He left school to train as an apprentice barber, but spent his teens playing semi-pro ball. Sold to the Cincinnati Reds at age 19, he became the youngest player in what was then the major league. Then, when the American League was just getting started, Crawford jumped his contract and signed with the Tigers, who were coming off a 52–83 season and were looking for a star.

Crawford wasn't regarded as one of the fastest players of his day, but in his day triples resulted from strength rather than speed. And Wahoo Sam was strong.

He didn't study the game, the way Cobb did. He would have fit in with later generations as a "see the ball, hit the ball" type of hitter.

"My idea of batting is a thing that should be done unconsciously," he once said. "If you get to studying it too much, to see just what fraction of a second you must swing to meet a curved ball, the chances are you will miss it altogether."

Crawford didn't miss it often. From 1905 to the end of his Tigers career in 1917, he never struck out more than 36 times in a season.

He was a star, the biggest and best-paid star before Cobb arrived. In fact, when the Tigers were touring the South to get ready for the 1904 season, Crawford was the player Cobb watched most closely when they passed through Augusta, Georgia. Crawford was the one he nervously approached after the game to ask advice on catching fly balls.

The two wouldn't get along nearly as well as teammates, with reports suggesting that the only time they spoke was when they were on the field, and then only when absolutely necessary.

"I spent 15 years in the same outfield with him," Crawford told the *Los Angeles Times* years later. "He never helped any of us with a loan, even when we were broke. And he had a rotten disposition, too."

Eventually, though, Cobb was one of those campaigning for Crawford to be enshrined in the Hall of Fame, an honor that finally arrived in 1957. Crawford fully deserved it, and not just because he had more triples than anyone who played the game.

But he does own that distinction.

The only way Crawford loses his triples record is if he keeps losing triples. New accounting has already cost him three since he died. Crawford's record was long listed at 312, before more careful reading of the records placed it at 309.

It hardly matters. Since 1917, when Crawford played his final major league game, no one has had even 200 career triples. Over the last half-century, only one player has even reached 150 (Roberto Clemente hit 166).

Forget catching Wahoo Sam. The way baseball is played today, no one is even getting halfway there.

MOST TRIPLES IN BASEBALL HISTORY

309
Sam Crawford

295
Ty Cobb

252
Honus Wagner

244
Jake Beckley

233
Roger Connor

222
Tris Speaker

Tigers'

4

Consecutive Division Titles

Yes, they want a ring. The current Tiger team doesn't have one yet, and some will never consider this group a success until the Tigers win it all.

That's fully understandable. Everyone in baseball works to win a World Series. Every baseball fan cheers in the hope of celebrating a World Series title.

It's also too bad, because the failure to win it all (yet) has overshadowed and lessened the credit for what the Tigers have accomplished over the last four years.

Four straight first-place finishes.

The St. Louis Cardinals, for all their championships, have never done that. The Los Angeles Dodgers haven't done it, and the Brooklyn Dodgers never did, either. The Boston Red Sox have never done it.

Only seven of baseball's 30 franchises have.

The Tigers never had, not until now. The '68 champions finished 19 games out the following year. The '84 champions finished 15 games out in 1985. The Ty Cobb Tigers went to the World Series three straight years from 1907 to 1909, but besides never winning one of them, they finished 18 games back in 1910, when they could have made it four in a row.

It's really not easy to finish on top four straight years, even if you have a financial advantage (which the current Tigers have had), and even if you play in a supposedly weak division (although the American League Central has also produced the AL's top wild-card team the last two seasons). It's really worth celebrating when you finish on top four straight years, even if four straight Octobers have ultimately brought disappointment to the Tigers and their fans.

For a moment, though, let's focus on what the 2011–14 Tigers did, rather than on what they didn't do.

They had a 95-win season in 2011, the year Justin Verlander won the Cy Young and the MVP. The Tigers started a little slow and didn't take over first place for good until the middle of July, but they went 46–24 after the All-Star break and clinched the division with nearly two weeks left to play. They beat the New York Yankees in the Division Series, but lost a tough ALCS to the Texas Rangers.

The 2012 Tigers had it tougher, even with Miguel Cabrera's Triple Crown season. The Tigers barely spent a day in first place until the final week of September. They were challenged by a surprisingly tough Chicago White Sox team, but repeated as division champions in large part because they won 12 of 18 head-to-head meetings with the Sox. The Tigers beat the Oakland A's in the Division Series and the Yankees in the ALCS, but were swept by the San Francisco Giants in the World Series.

The 2013 team nearly went wire-to-wire, spending 158 days in first place. But the 2013 Tigers also nearly blew it at the end, going 13–13 in September while the Cleveland Indians were going 21–6. The Tigers ended up needing every one of their 93 wins, because the Indians won 92, including the final 10 games in a row. Once again, though, the Tigers were at their best against their closest pursuers, finishing 15–4 against the Tribe. Once again, the Tigers got through the Division Series (again against the A's) before losing in the ALCS (this time to the Boston Red Sox).

The plan was that 2014 would be different, and not just because Jim Leyland retired as manager and the Tigers hired Brad Ausmus to replace him. It was different, but only in that the ride felt even rougher. The end result was the same, both over 162 games (90 wins and another division title) and in October (disappointment with a first-round sweep by the Baltimore Orioles). Once again, the Tigers faced a serious challenge, this time from the Kansas City Royals. Once again, they came out on top, in large part because they did so well (13–6) in head-to-head meetings with that top challenger.

The streak lives on, and the Tigers will try to make it five in a row in 2015. Only four franchises have finished first five seasons in a row. Only two (the Yankees from 1998 to 2006 and the Braves from 1995 to 2005) have been on top more than five straight years.

It's not easy. Teams change, players get hurt, performances vary, and luck factors in. It's not easy, but it is impressive, because everyone can agree that the 162-game schedule provides a far better measuring stick for a baseball team than a best-of-five or best-of-seven series.

We care more about those short series, and perhaps that's as it should be. Everyone dreams of hitting the home run that wins the World Series, not the one that wins the Central.

When the 2015 season begins, it will have been 31 years since the Tigers and their fans last enjoyed the joy that comes from a World Series title. But it will also have been five years since the last time the Tigers didn't finish a regular season in first place.

Maybe that's not much of a consolation prize. Maybe it shouldn't feel like one.

It's still quite an accomplishment.

Ernie Harwell's

6,000

(or So) Games
Calling the Tigers

His first game went 15 innings.

It was in Cleveland, and it was cold. Really cold. About 35 degrees with a biting wind, as Ernie Harwell would remember it years later. He was sitting in the upper deck at old Municipal Stadium, because in 1960 the Indians didn't have a broadcast booth for George Kell and the new guy who had worked before in Baltimore.

Van Patrick was gone, because the Tigers changed beer sponsors that winter, and Patrick's close association with Goebel's beer didn't suit Stroh's, the new sponsor. Kell played in Baltimore when Harwell was broadcasting Orioles games, and so he suggested the Tigers might want to hire the young guy with the smooth Georgia accent.

So there they were on Opening Day 1960, in a game that got much more attention because the Tigers and Indians had just made the Harvey Kuenn for Rocky Colavito trade.

And it was cold.

"All I wanted to do and all George wanted to do from the first pitch was get back to the hotel," Harwell would tell author Tom Keegan years later.

They were sitting at that table in the upper deck. It was Ernie Harwell's first day in the Tiger broadcast booth, and he didn't even have a booth.

The years would go on, the conditions would get better, and Harwell would be much more known for the warmth of his voice than for the cold of that very first day on the job. And as for that game that just kept going, perhaps it was a sign, because Harwell's career with the Tigers would just keep going, even after they fired him.

They fired Ernie Harwell?

Yes, they did, and it sounds just as shocking today as it did on that December day in 1990, when Harwell announced it himself. Yes, he announced his own firing.

He would come back a year later, brought back as one of Mike Ilitch's first acts after buying the team from Tom Monaghan. He would return to the radio booth in an uneasy partnership with Rick Rizzs and Bob Rathbun, then for a few years on television, then finally back in the radio booth with Jim Price and Dan Dickerson.

He would finally leave on his own terms, announcing his own retirement this time, deciding that his 42nd year broadcasting the Tigers would be his last. He signed off in Toronto after the final game of the 2002 season, reading a short thank you note to his listeners.

"It's time to say goodbye, but I think goodbyes are sad and I'd much rather say hello," Harwell said that day. "Hello to a new adventure."

He was 84 years old, and he was talking new adventures. He was 84 years old, and we were still asking him, "Why now?"

Ernie Harwell stands near a statue honoring him inside the entrance to Comerica Park. *(Photo Courtesy AP Photo/Paul Sancya)*

Tiger fans have grown comfortable with Dickerson and Price, who carried on in the radio booth after Harwell's retirement. They've come to associate television broadcasters Mario Impemba and Rod Allen with this new era of Tiger success.

But even now, even 13 years after his retirement and five years after he died, there's still some feeling of surprise and regret when you turn on the Tigers in the summer and Ernie isn't there.

He was always there, through the '60s and the '70s and the '80s. He was always there, from the days of Kaline to the days of Tram and Lou to the days of Bobby Higginson.

He's still there, in spirit. An Ernie Harwell statue stands at one of the entrances to Comerica Park, where the press box is known as the Ernie Harwell Media Center.

It's hard to find any record of exactly how many Tiger games Harwell called, but even a rough estimate will overwhelm you. He often said that he missed only two games during all his years, one for his brother's funeral in 1968 and the other when he went into the National Sportscasters and Sportswriters Hall of Fame in 1989.

The Tigers played 6,184 regular-season games during Harwell's 42 seasons. They played 13 playoff games and 12 World Series games. And Harwell would call a handful of spring training games, beginning every spring by "talking about the turtle," as generations in Michigan came to know his annual recitation of the "Song of the Turtle."

But there were also four seasons in the mid-1990s when Harwell was working for PASS, the cable television company that broadcast Tiger games. PASS didn't carry the entire schedule, so there were games in those seasons that Harwell didn't call.

So let's just say it was 6,000 (or so). Let's just say that the exact number doesn't matter, that if you turned on a radio in Michigan anywhere from 1960 to 2002, there was a better than decent chance you were going to hear Ernie Harwell's voice.

And an even better chance that you would like it.

Acknowledgments

I've been around for quite a bit of Tiger history, but not nearly all of it. So when the good people at Triumph asked me about doing this book, I knew I was going to need some help.

Thankfully, Dan Ewald and Jim Hawkins were available, both with stories they've told me and with the books they have written. Thankfully, I'd spent 18 years on the beat with Tom Gage, Gene Guidi, and John Lowe, who were around for even more Tiger history than I was. Thankfully, George Cantor wrote outstanding books about both the 1968 and 1984 championship teams, and there have also been outstanding books written about or by Ty Cobb, Hank Greenberg, Hughie Jennings, Charlie Gehringer, Mickey Cochrane, Bill Lajoie, Ernie Harwell, Denny McLain, and Armando Galarraga.

The SABR Biography Project was also a great resource, as were the online archives of the *Detroit News, Detroit Free Press, New York Times,* and my old employer, Booth Newspapers. And then there's baseball-reference.com. This book could never have been finished without the indispensable website created by Sean Forman, who has revolutionized baseball reporting and research.

Thanks to current and former Tigers who took time to help me. I worked with great Tiger managers, and much of what I know about baseball came from Sparky Anderson and Jim Leyland. Jim Price, Rod Allen, John McHale, Jerry Walker, Mike Maroth, Justin Verlander, Curtis Granderson, Anibal Sanchez, and Jeff Jones all helped with personal memories specifically for this book.

Thanks also to all the people I worked with at Booth, from Larry McDermott to Meegan Holland to Tim Gillman to Andy Flanagan to Mary Ullmer, and the late Dennis Tanner. And most of all, there's still not a day that goes by that I don't think of Vern Plagenhoef, who served as friend and mentor in the too-short time we worked together.

Thanks to Tom Bast, Jesse Jordan, et al at Triumph, and to my good friend Jayson Stark, who helped bring us together. Also to Jon Heyman and Scott Miller, who were my colleagues at CBSSports. com and remain two of my closest friends. And to my ever-supportive family, my parents, my brother Mike, and especially Lek, who was always patient when I told her I still had to "tahm ngahn on the book."

Sources

Alexander, Charles C. *Ty Cobb*. Oxford University Press. 1984.

Anderson, Sparky, with Dan Ewald. *They Call Me Sparky*. Sleeping Bear Press. 1998.

Bak, Richard. *Cobb Would Have Caught It: The Golden Age of Baseball in Detroit*. Wayne State University Press. 1993

Cantor, George. *The Tigers of '68: Baseball's Last Real Champions*. Taylor Trade Publishing. 1997.

Cantor, George. *Wire to Wire: Inside the 1984 Detroit Tigers Championship Season*. Triumph Books. 2004.

Cantor, George. *The Good, the Bad & the Ugly: Detroit Tigers: Heart-Pounding, Jaw-Dropping and Gut-Wrenching Moments from Detroit Tigers History*. Triumph Books. 2008.

Cochrane, Mickey. *Baseball: The Fan's Game*. SABR Digital Library. 2014.

Craig, Roger, with Vern Plagenhoef. *Inside Pitch: Roger Craig's '84 Tiger Journal*. Wm. B. Eerdmans Publishing. 1984.

Galarraga, Armando and Joyce, Jim, with Daniel Paisner. *Nobody's Perfect: Two Men, One Call, and a Game for Baseball History*. Atlantic Monthly Press. 2011.

Handrinos, Peter. *Baseball Men: The Comeback*. http://angels.scout.com/2/586736.html.

Hawkins, Jim. *Al Kaline: The Biography of a Tigers Icon*. Triumph Books. 2010.

Hawkins, Jim and Ewald, Dan. *The Detroit Tigers Encyclopedia*. Sports Publishing. 2003.

Keegan, Tom. *Ernie Harwell: My 60 Years in Baseball*. Triumph Books. 2005.

Kell, George, with Dan Ewald. *Hello Everybody, I'm George Kell*. Sports Publishing. 1998.

Kurlansky, Mark. *Hank Greenberg: The Hero Who Didn't Want to Be One.* Yale University Press. 2011.

Lidz, Franz. "Hank Greenberg didn't have a last shot in the dark at Ruth's record." *Sports Illustrated,* June 14, 1982.

McLain, Denny, with Eli Zaret. *I Told You I Wasn't Perfect.* Triumph Books. 2007.

Ritter, Lawrence S. *The Glory of Their Times: The Story of the Early Days of Baseball Told by the Men Who Played It.* Harper Perennial. 1966.

Rosen, Dick. "Rev. Aloysius Travers, S.J.: The Hawk Who Became a Tiger for a Day." Philadelphia Athletics Historical Society. 2010.

Sinha, Anup and Lajoie, Bill. *Character Is Not a Statistic: The Legacy and Wisdom of Baseball's Godfather Scout, Bill Lajoie.* Xlibris, Corp. 2010.

Skipper, John C. *Charlie Gehringer: A Biography of the Hall of Fame Tigers Second Baseman.* McFarland. 2008.

Smiles, Jack. *"Ee-Yah": The Life and Times of Hughie Jennings, Baseball Hall of Famer.* McFarland. 2005.

Smith, Burge Carmon. *The 1945 Detroit Tigers: Nine Old Men and One Young Left Arm Win It All.* McFarland. 2010.

Society for American Baseball Research. *The SABR Baseball List and Record Book: Baseball's Most Fascinating Records and Unusual Statistics.* Scribner. 2007.

Stewart, Art, with Sam Mellinger. *The Art of Scouting: Seven Decades Chasing Hopes and Dreams in Major League Baseball.* Ascend Books. 2014.

Stewart, Mark. *Pitching to the Pennant: The 1954 Cleveland Indians.* University of Nebraska Press. 2014.

Stump, Al. *Cobb: A Biography.* Algonquin Books. 1996.